F. B Coffin

Coffin's Poems

F. B Coffin

Coffin's Poems

ISBN/EAN: 9783744705103

Printed in Europe, USA, Canada, Australia, Japan

Cover: Foto ©Thomas Meinert / pixelio.de

More available books at **www.hansebooks.com**

COFFIN'S POEMS

with

Ajax' Ordeals

by

F. B. Coffin

LITTLE ROCK, ARKANSAS:
The Colored Advocate, Printers and Binders.
1897.

Dedicated

To the memory
Of that angelic woman,
  Who claimed me as her son;
Of that majestic woman,
  Whose race on earth was run—
Long before I was old enough,
  To reason right from wrong;
Long before I listened to
  Redemption's saving song.
Of that Christ loving woman,
  Who's now at Jesus' home,
Who sits and talks with angels,
  And with archangels roam.

SECOND.

To the conscience of the nation,
  With the hopes that it may rise
To the point of elevation
  That will open up its eyes,
And lend to us a list'ning ear,
  For the pitiful tale of woe,
That Ajax* cannot sleep at night
  For lynchers are aglow.

They burn poor Ajax at the stake,
    They hang him to a tree;
They chop him up like sausage meat,
    From home they make him flee.

*The latter part of this volume will explain
who Ajax is.

Preface.

Brief is our life here, precious is the time, and great the work to do, and a few thoughts in print has the possibility of a longer life than a man. "The night cometh when no man can work."

How sweet, if it might be, that when the day is ended, we may have left some watch words still ringing in the ears of those who come after us. And I may be permitted to hope that these meditations may have such power, in their modest way. They will be easily passed by but may have a message for hearts that will look and listen.

There is, certainly in this age, a want of writing that shall rest and brace the mind. It is well to extend natural and spontaneous thoughts, especially that which the heart has laid by in store. We must be militant here on earth, militant against every form of error.

If, during the period of American Slavery, any Anglo-Saxon raised his voice or moved his pen in the interest of the stolen and oppressed African, that man was marked, reviled and ostracised as if he was affected with the leprosy. No historian could write a true re-

In this age ideal frivolity supersedes stern reality. In most of our large cities in the South—outside of the college societies—there are no permanent, genuine literary organizations among our so called intelligent people for elevation.

They meet socially with no definite purpose to social elevation. They meet religiously with their souls on fashion and God as secondary. They never meet intellectually. These talents grow up in thorns and thistles. Nothing to inspire our youths to merit. Position, irrespective to character or ability, reigns supreme. Thousands of youths grow up under this poisonous atmosphere in the large cities. But it is encouraging to see that, from the smaller towns, the college walls(our safeguards) are filled with youths preparing themselves to meet the demands of future times.

What is the worth of fashion, style, and social ethics if it does not add to the world better, nobler, truer, sounder, more reliable men from its factory? Time will not attempt to test their logic but will, eventually, weigh the results.   AUTHOR.

At My Mother's Grave.

I never see the burial place,
Where my dear mother lies;
But that I think I see her face,
Peak at me through the skies.

I stand around her sacred mound,
And think she knows I'm there;
I kneel upon the sacred ground
And lisp her evening prayer.

Her fav'rite hymn I then repeat,
With accents all her own;
We seem to meet at Jesus' feet,
And linger near His throne.

She sleeps within her narrow cot,
Safe "tucked in" from the night;
Resigned, I leave the solemn spot,
"God doeth all things right."

What an hour it must have been
    For a woman's tender heart,
When the pityless, rough lynchers,
    Tore she'nd her husband apart.

And while the mother clasped her hands
    And the children wept and prayed;
The whole family made struggles,
    And shrieked to heaven for aid.

The atrocities of Russia
    Against the thriving Jew,
And the horrors of Liberia,
    Would disappear from view.

Mob violence against China,
    And all the heathen lands;
Is far surpassed by lynch law,
    In this, our Southern land.

If we ask ourselves the question
    "Why do they lynch the Negro?"
Our hearts respond full sadly,
    "They, nor we, do not know."

We've asked the wise in every age,
    And searched the universe around;
But neither scientist nor sage,
    An answer to the quest has found.

Is it God's will, what seer can tell?
  (Thus do our anxious thoughts revolve)
Or is there not some oracle,
  That can or will the problem solve?

Are we but phantoms, with no cause,
  But chance from cradle to the grave;
Or those inexorable laws
  Of which agnostics boast and rave?

Or are we orphans with no home,
  With none whom we can father call;
As outcasts here a while to roam,
  And then pass off with "death ends all?"

No! let us not discouraged be
  But hope and ever pray
That wrong and inhumanity,
  May cease to be some day.

While the storms of life are raging
  Lynching wild in our land,
Can we find a better refuge
  Than the shadow of God's hand?

But what shall cleanse our country
  From all this painful guilt,
The blood of freemen shed by freemen,
  Upon her bosom spilt?

When the pilgrim fathers came
　　From far across the sea;
Their purposes were nobler than
　　The lynching of the free.

When Washington at Valley Forge
　　Endured the winter's pain,
And when he crossed the Deleware
　　'Twas all for freedom's name.

He knew not that a cent'ry hence,
　　The flag for which he fought;
Would be disgraced by lynching men,
　　By taking life for naught.

When Lincoln gave that mighty stroke,
　　When Sherman reached the sea,
When Grant took Appomatax,
　　Their cry was liberty.

When John Brown laid his body down
　　And his soul went marching on,
He knew not that his cause would be
　　Disgraced by this great wrong.

Could these great men speak back today
　　From their resting domain;
They'd whisper all in one accord,
　　"Our blood was spilt in vain."

Dear native land, a newer page
  Must turn as time moves by;
Shall that page be brighter,
  Or shall thy greatness die?

Thou hast a noble government,
  And 'tis with trembling heart,
That we see what thou appearest
  And look on what thou art.

We've wept till we could not weep,
  And the pain of our burning eyes
Has gone into our aching hearts,
  And now the nation cries.

Earth uplifts a general cry,
  For all this guilt and wrong;
And heaven's ears are listening
  To the suff'rers' wailing song.

Who'll interpret this mystery?
  Even the common dust
Under the feet of the guilty
  Cries out "this crime's unjust."

But we shall see the day,
  When right shall surely reign;
When at the bar of conscience,
  The guilty shall be slain.

2

*   *   *   *

It may be when Ida Wells' lessons have been
    learned
The lynchers sun forever more has set,
The things which our weak judgment here have
    spurned,
The things o'er which we've grieved with lash-
    es wet,
Will flash before them out of life's dark night
As stars shine most in deeper tints of blue.
And they shall see how all her plans were right
And how what seemed reproof was love most
    true;
And when those nations far across the sea
Begin to point o'er here the finger of shame,
And show our state the depth of all these
    crimes,
I think she will take steps to stop the same.

You know that prudent parents disallow
Too much of sweet to craving babyhood;
So God, perhaps, is holding from us now
Life's sweetest things because it seemeth good,
And they shall shortly know that lengthened
    breath
Is not the sweetest gift God sends His friends,

And that sometimes the sable pall of death
Conceals the fairest boon His love can send.
And if through all this strife we live to stand
Where our minds from lynching news may rest,
Then we shall clearly know and understand;
I think that all will say "God knew the best."

Only.

Only Afric's jungles
   Satisfied his mind,
While the happy Negro
   On his couch reclined.

Only a human trading ship
   Coasting along the shore,
The Negro knew not whither
   Still he had to go.

Only a "Star Spangled banner,"
   The Negro saw it wave,
But he saw not "land of free"
   Neither "home of brave."

Only slavery's hardships
   The Negro bore for years,
On through the wilderness
   With headaches and tears.

Only John Brown's body
  Is moulding in the clay,
Yet his soul is marching,
  Showing us the way.

Only Bull Run's battle,
  Up sprang General Grant,
Four long years of bloodshed,
  Freedom was the chant.

Only Abraham Lincoln
  Gave the mighty stroke,
And four million Negroes
  Lost the slavish yoke.

Only an education,
  That is what he wants,
And to be a citizen
  But they say he can't.

Only abiding by the law
  Of our God and man,
And on all public questions
  For the right, he tries to stand.

Only to suit the appetites
  Of other wicked men,
Our race is mobb'd and lynch'd
  Isn't that a sin?

Only proud America
    Detests human strife,
Still has not courage to
    Protect human life.

Only that coming day,
    'Pointed hour make haste,
She must stand 'fore her God,
    Past that solemn test.

Mother's Songs.

The summer's sun was beaming hot,
    The boys had played all day;
And now beside a rippling stream,
    Upon the grass they lay.

Tired of games and idle jest,
    As swept the hours along,
They called on one who mused at times,
    "Come pard, give us a song."

"I fear I cannot please," he said,
    "The only songs I know
Are those my mother used to sing
    To me long years ago."

"Sing one of those," a rough voice said,
"There's none but true men here;
To ev'ry mother's son of us
A mother's song is dear."

Then sweetly rose the singer's voice,
Amid unwonted calm:
"Am I a soldier of the cross
A follower of the lamb."

"And shall I fear to own his cause"
Every heart seemed stilled,
And hearts that never throbbed with fear,
With tender thoughts were filled.

As the singer closed he said,
" Boys, we must face the foes"
Then thanking them for their invite
Upon his feet he rose.

" Sing us one more the young men said,
The singer hung his head,
Then glancing 'round with smiling lips,
"You'll join with me," he said.

We'll sing that old familiar air,
Sweet as the bugle call;
"All hail the power of Jesus name,
Let Angels prostrate fall."

And wondrous was the old tune's spell,
  As on the singer sang;
Man after man fell into line,
  And loud their voices rang.

One cried out "my mother sings
  'Just as I am though tossed about;' "
And the crowd picked up the anthem—
  "With many a conflict, many a doubt."

The next said "I seem to hear,
  'It's rock of ages cleft for me,' "
And the boys joined in with feeling
  "Let me hide myself in thee."

Another said "I'm an outcast,
  But when I've nowhere to roam,
I think of mother and the city
  Which, long since she's made her home."

The next one said with tearful eyes
  "My mother's in eternity,
Her song was 'O rock of ages
  In thy cleft hide thou me.' "

Hush'd are her lips, the song's ended,
  The singer sleeps at last;
While I sit here in deep wonder,
  And think of days, long past.

The room still echoes with music,
   As singing soft and low,
Those grand sweet Christian carols,
   They rock her too and fro.

Safe hidden in the "Rock of Ages"
   She bade farewell to fear;
Sure that her Lord'd always lead her
   "She read her title clear."

Dear Saint in mansions long folded,
   Safe in God's fostering love,
She joins in the blissful chorus,
   Of those bright choirs above.

There she knows not pain, nor sorrow,
   Safe beyond Jordan's roll
She lives with her blessed Jesus
   The lover of her soul.

These boys are men, the stream still runs,
   Those songs, they still are heard;
And oh! the depth of every soul,
   By those old hymns is stirred.

And up from many a bearded lip,
   In whispers soft and low;
Rises the songs the mother taught
   The boy long years ago.

Spotless.

(James 1:21)

Spotless, spotless, spotless, spotless,
   At the sounding of that word,
All my soul turned up to heaven,
   All my heart within me stirred.

Would that I could stand out spotless,
   Lord, I know that Thou hast died,
Thou hast stood for ages spotless
   Bidding men come and abide.

Lord, build up for me a ladder,
   Reaching into perfect day,
That my hopes this word may grapple,
   Showing me the right of way.

Blooming flowers all seem spotless,
   On the spotless hill and dell,
Oh, how beautiful they all are,
   And how fragrant too they smell.

The spotless birds, they spring along,
   And chirp the song of jubilee;
I like to hear their spotless songs,
   They make my melancholy flee.

I wish that I could so be found,
　While traveling life's brief way,
A spotless light to every one,
　Where'er my footsteps stray.

Once a woman tried to show me
　Something spotless, bright and new,
And she pick'd for illustration
　Objects of the dirtiest hue.

"Lady" said I, eager, anxious,
"Why do you choose things so vile?"
"Just to show the cleansing process,"
　Said the lady with a smile.

Then she said "these dirty colors,
　Hardest to remove of all,
Can be made by constant rubbing
　White as snowflake in its fall."

These words struck my heart with power,
　Made my soul within me throb,
"Dirty colors"—"white as snowflake"
　Can this woman?　Cannot God?

Lord, I long to be made spotless,
　What lack I to make me thine?
Not in name but spotless truly,
　Would I have thy ways, not mine.

Is there anything not spotless
　That I cherish more than Thee,
Loved ones, money, fame or talent?
　Lord reveal them now to me.

Lord I think how Thou, though spotless,
　Left thy Heavenly home on high,
Gave up all Thy spotless glory,
　Came to earth for us, to die.

Jesus spoke from out His mansion:
　"Thou, as I, can spotless be,
Vilest hearts have been made precious,
　Simply trust and follow me."
Then I cried, "O Jesus take me,
　Give me spotless, crimson wings,
Stamp my name upon thy roll book,
　Take it to the spotless King."

　　　*　　*　　*　　*

Oh, what spotless, rapturous music!
　Heaven's gates seemed open wide,
And I stood there clear and spotless,
　Near the Saviour's spotless side.

Spotless in God's spotless mansions!
　Spotless in His spotless light!
　God's own love, majestic, spotless,
Made me crimson, spotless white!

Motherly Emotions.

A mother* came passing by my door,
  Her son was near by my side;
"Howdy mama" was her son's adore,
  "Howdy my son" she replied.

And as I gazed upon that mother,
  The tears rushed to my eyes;
My heart's affections began to swell,
  My mind went to paradise.

While there it found that one model,
  Who, sixteen long years ago,
By the blessed Saviour's command,
  Left all earth's sorrows below.

"What word is sweeter than mother,
  What place is dearer than home?"
These words are our associates
  Wherever in life we roam.

Napoleon was a worldly man,
  Yet one great thing he uttered,
When from conscience clear he said,
  "What France most needs is mothers."

Home, that sanctuary of love,
   That stamps impressions for life,
Who's the heart of affection there?
   It is the mother, the wife.

A mother's love! oh, no one knows
   How much of life's feelings lies,
In those sweet words, the fears, the hopes,
   And daily strengthening ties.

It wakes ere yet the infant dreams
   It's earliest vital breath;
And fails but when the mother's heart
   Chills in the grasp of death.

Who knows the worth of mother?
   Not those who see her daily;
But those who watch that vacant chair
   Whose days are dark and dreary.

But when I am tossed and driven,
   And feel like I'm all alone;
I think of mother and that city,
   Which long since she's made her home.

Mother, while playing at thy knees,
   Within my youthful heart;
There dwelt no secret consciousness,
   That thou would e'er depart.

Since thou hast gone I now have learned
  To bow my stubborn will,
The power that calms the raging sea
  My rebel heart has stilled.

So I can look with fearless eyes
  On all these earthly fates,
But how coulds't thou afford to die
  And leave me desolate?

I should not weep for thee, dear one,
  While with the saints thou art,
But how can I in coldness check
  The burning tears that start?

My thoughts to thee must ever turn
  As in my infant days,
While in my heart thine image shall
  Lead me through life's rough ways.

Rest, dearest one, may angel host
  Their vigils o'er thee keep,
How can I breath thy saintly name
  And yet forbear to weep?

I stand heartbroken on dull earth
  And gaze on the vacant skies,
Mother I cannot see thy face,
  Dost thou hear thy son's cry?

If in God's likeness I may awake
And shine in pure image by thee,
I'll be satisfied when I can break
The fetters of flesh and be free.

*Mrs. L. E. S.

Consolation.

Friends can't you tell me something?
I am weary and worn tonight.
The day has gone like a shadow
And only the evening is light.

Tell me about the Master,
Of the burdensome hills he trod,
When the tears and blood from his an-
guish
Dropped down on Judea's sod.

Tell me about the Master,
Of the wrongs he freely forgave,
Of His love and His tender compassion,
Of His love that is mighty to save.

For my heart is restless and weary
Of the woes and temptations of life,
Of all the treacherous conflicts
Of falsehood, and malice, and strife.

So tell me the sweet old story
    That falls on each wound like a balm,
And my heart now bruised and broken,
    Shall grow patient, strong, and calm.

Life What We Make It.

My life is a wearisome journey;
    I'm sick with the times and the heat,
The rays of the sun beat upon me;
    Life's briars are wounding my feet.

There are so many hills leading upwards
    It keeps me a longing for rest,
But he who appoints me my journey,
    Knows just what is needful and best.

He loves me too well to forsake me,
    Or give me one trial too much,
And the toils of my road will seem noth-
        ing
    When e'er I receive his kind touch.

When the last feeble step has been taken
    And the gates of the city appear,
The beautiful songs of the angels
    Will float out on listening ears.

Though now I am foot-sore and weary,
I'll rest when I'm safely at home,
I know I'll receive a glad welcome
For the Saviour Himself has said: "come."

So when I am weary in body
And sinking in spirit, I say,
All the toils of the road will seem noth-
ing
When I get to the end of the way.

Then I'll try to press hopefully on-
ward,
Thinking often through each weary day,
The toils of the road will seem nothing
When I get to the end of my way.

Frances E. Harper.
Tribute.

Dear friend, to me one vision craved,
Alas! has been denied;
But thy strong words on page of book
My mind anew inspires,
Thy noble soul has lifted mine,
As rippling waves are drawn;
My spirit heard thy words sublime,
About the woman's dawn.

3

Some mysteries of Afric's race,
    Were left for thee to prove;
Thy lucid voice, thy pen of grace,
    Filled up with hope and love—
Woke the dead pulse of joy supreme,
    In our discouraged hearts,
Dispells the long delusive dream,
    Makes new ambitions start.

The rebels who pronounce us brutes,
    With conscience all at rest;
Feel the great throb of Afric's truth,
    That stirs from out thy breast;
Maid of a higher, nobler cause,
    Thou queen of ancient night;
Defender of the virtuous laws
    Of our young woman's rights.

Thy name has spread like night's domain,
    When all her glittering lamps
Illume the vast and level plains
    Into the peaceful camps—
Where martyrs keep the righteous post
    Doubting our freedom yet,
And speed the faithful, onward host,
    With eyes on justice set.

They are not dead, those who have died,
　Like holy angels come
To mortals in their faithful strides
　For country, love and home;
Thou knowest the psalms by sages
　　　wrought,
　Through shaky, mythic phrase;
Thou nobler psalms than they have taught,
　Yet they have all the praise.

The time will come when this great state,
　With conscience clear and true,
Will feel the strain of human fate,
　Revealed to them by you;
And from her high esteemed estate,
　She will throw open wide
The portal of her royal gate,
　So long to us denied.

Continue in thy noble work,
　O, faithful sister great,
Until thy mind redeeming words,
　Are spread in every state;
Bring womanhood her honors due,
　Heal up these long disgraces;
The time has come when woman must
　March out and lead the races.

Cain and Abel.

"To thine ownself be true,
And it must follow as the night the day,
Thou canst not then be false to any man."

Cain was not true to Abel,
    Neither true to himself,
Because Abel was true to both,
    He put his brother to death.

I think how many a hundred
    Of innocent Negro men.
Each trying to do like Abel,
    Have died his death since then.

Voice From The South.

To Mrs. Annie Julia Cooper.

I read that book, "Voice from the South,"
    I read it o'er again;
I re-read, heart leaped up to mouth
    At its triumphant aim.

It 'rouses those noble feelings,
    Which partly are obscure;
It makes us see as we are seen,
    And fits us to endure.

It pictures a steadfast purpose,
  A brave and daring will,
A human-needed promise that
  We hope the years will fill.

Noble woman, grandly gifted,
  Sent to tell the world true facts;
Sure the race will be uplifted
  By thy words, thy deeds, thy acts.

Thy dauntless words are great and bold,
  At times they seem to be—
Like John Brown's in dark slavery's days,
  While battling for the free.

Earth's grandest hearts uplift to thee,
  They feel thy spreading fame;
And children that are yet to be
  Will "hallowed be thy name."

From thy book, those worthy pages,
  All our anxious hearts entreat;
All true trophies of the ages,
  Are enshrined at thy dear feet.

Oh! wished for, hoped for, happy time,
  When I can have the grace,
To grasp thy hand, and more sublime,
  Upon thy statue gaze.

When e'er I 'tempt to write of thee,
  Love takes my thoughts away;
Thy dazzling fame makes all that flee,
  Which most I long to say.

If thou hadst hearing in thy heart,
  To know how others beat;
Then thou shouldst walk where'er thou art,
  Where throbbing millions greet.

O ye whose noble, lucid pen,
  Forever filled with ink;
To touch the hearts and minds of men,
  And make whole nations think.

It may be that in this cold world,
  You will be ostracised
For noble truths which you have hurled
  At those who right despise.

But Christ was ostracised by men,
  He conquered every one;
Brave Luther faced the Papal den,
  And he the victory won.

So while within this vale of tears,
  Where sins and woes are rife;
Thy words will prove, in coming years,
  The gift of mortal-life.

Since we are scattered as a race,
　　And thou hast power to write;
While God prolongs thy days of grace,
　　Cry to the race "unite."

Thou hast been writing, noble one,
　　Thou dost not write in vain;
Thy words, methink, are pressing on,
　　They shall be entertained.

Thy writing has a dwelling place,
　　Above this lynching ken;
We hope thy spirit will never trace
　　Such wicked haunts of men.

In some far off diviner land,
　　There stands a giant Mast;
It waves to you a cheering hand,
　　From heroes of the past.

Thy 'lectric voice, whose strong control,
　　As with an angel's breath
Can stir the fountain of the soul,
　　And cheer the long bereft.

Write on, and may thy words still strike
　　The conscience of the nation;
Ar d show that all men are alike,
　　And have been since creation.

Bishop Daniel A. Payne.
(Deceased).

He has gone forth in the light of light,
Out of the long watch and the heavy night,
Out of the life that was so hard to bear,
Crowded by sorrow and perplexed by care.

Love was the life which pulsed his being
    through,
No task too hard, if set by love to do,
No pain too sharp, if love called to endure,
No weariness he knew if love was true.

Heaven has received him as a welcome guest,
Balming earth's tie with compensating rest,
Healing earth's grievous wound with sure
    content,
The sense of home after long banishment.

But more to him than smile of vanished kin,
Or hands outstreched to greet and draw him
    in,
Or "bonded walls" of amethyst unpriced
Is the clear vision of the face of Christ.

The face divine, which, in his boyhood days,
Seeing he loved and never looked away,
Which, like a star in the dim firmament,
Guided his steps and moved where'er he went.

Out of the life that was not always sweet,
Out of the puzzle and the day's defeat,
Out of earth's hindering and alien zone,
The Lord of love has led him to his own.

Douglass Dead?

Across the nation's broad domain,
On every hill, and every plain,
Peals out the muffled, sad refrain,
    That Douglass is dead.

O no, not dead! for every heart
In every state must surely start
As freedom's great, uprising mart,
    If Douglass is dead!

And far across the deep blue sea,
Those nations that love liberty,
Their minds will be a mournful lea,
    For Douglass' death.

Once freedom's great, uprising host,
From Maine to California's coast,
Of this great man could truly boast,
    And now he's dead!

In every heart of all the race,
He'll ever have a sacred place,
His name can never be erased,
     He is not dead!

He's with Lincoln, John Brown, Grant,
With Bishop Payne and Price he chants,
With such surrounding host we can't
     Say he is dead!

The Easter Man.

So crushed by sinful oppression,
     Through the ages long and drear,
Men began to doubt and question,
     Whether Shiloh would appear.

The Jewish doctors pondered,
     And Gentile sages dreamed,
While on their weary vision
     No assuring light yet gleamed.

But while time's dial was still moving,
     God, in a mysterious way,
Let man go in his wonder,
     He knew the time and the day.

And the Watchman he stood mourning,
  Over Judah's seer that day;
As up on Bethlehem's hillside,
  They wound their weary way.

And the watchman cried "O Israel,
  How long are we to stand,
Under the great oppressor's yoke,
  To be moved by Shiloh's hand?"

When heaven and earth were silent,
  When the Lord's will would be done,
The cry went from out Bethlehem,
  "A man child there is born."

Then burst the rapturous anthem;
  "Glory to God be given,
Good will among the sons of Men
  Peace on earth and in heaven."

While there in his manger cradle,
  The unconscious monarch lay,
The babe of Bethlehem now born,
  To have universal sway.

The human sea became restless,
  Earth's kingdoms began to shake,
And the universal cry was
  "Never man like that man spake."

When He began his active work,
  For three long toilsome years,
He climbed degradation's mountain,
  Wading through heart-aches and tears.

But Jesus buried these sorrows,
  Knowing the world had its share;
He opened a crystal fountain,
  To wash away sinful snares.

The more he spread his mission,
  The more he became despised,
He forgave men this wickedness,
  And yet he was crucified.

Nineteen centuries have passed and gone,
  Since " it is finished" was cried,
Every day during that time,
  The Savior's been crucified.

If we ask ourselves the question,
  " Why crucify one so dear?"
Our hearts will respond full sadly,
  " The answer is not here."

The still, small voice from Calvary
  Cries " I did all this for thee,"
And from the ear of faith we hear,
  " What art thou doing for me·"

Silence reigned in Jerusalem, -
   Men became bothered in mind,
Questions were asked about Jesus,
   To answer wise men declined.

On that lovely Easter morning,
   Mary and others came near,
The angel solved the mystery,
   "He's risen, He is not here."

He spent forty days sojourning,
   To many he made himself known,
He told of a city called Heaven,
   Entreated them to make it their home.

He melted down satan's mansions,
   He made intercession for man,
He gave his peace to the nations,
   And gave the disciples command.

And then along the silent path,
   By viewless spirits trod,
He left the blights of this sad earth,
   And went to dwell with God.

Gates of Heaven all stood ajar,
   Bells of Heaven were ringing,
Angels stood around the gate,
   Waiting. watching, singing.

And as the Savior entered in,
  They did not close the view,
But left the gate standing ajar
  That we might enter too.

Heaven's orchestra uttered aloud,
  "Worthy the Lamb that was slain
To receive honor, glory, power,
  Blessings, world without end."

For every thorn that gave a wound,
  A rose in Heaven was given,
And joy, that there no roses found
  With rosy wreaths were riven.

In paradise where breezes blow,
  To cool the heart's hot fever,
The pangs and pain He felt below,
  Were waft away forever.

*   *   *   *   *

To look at Thee, O Lord, as Thou art,
  From this mortal perishing clay,
The spirit immortal in peace would de-
    part,
  And joyous mount up her bright way.

I know our stained tablets must first be
    washed white,
  To let Thy bright features be drawn.
We know we must suffer the darkness of
    night,
  To welcome the coming of dawn.

But we shall be satisfied when we can
    cast
  The shadow of nature all by,
When the cold, heavy world from our
    vision has passed
  To let the soul open her eye.
We come together in Easter service,
  To sing praises unto His name.
Let every day be Easter in which
  We will sing His praises the same.

Man's Imperfections.

O life why so imperfect?
  And life cried in elation,
Don't fault my God nor me correct,
  But man and his ovation.

The little bird enjoys his life,
　　The ant improves his time;
Its only man's abusive strife,
　　That wrecks this holy clime.

The rippling stream goes swiftly by,
　　The plants grow undistubed;
And only man fills life with sighs,
　　And makes crime reign superb.

The sun and moon and stars are bright,
　　This earth's a paradise;
But man stands in his own sunlight,
　　As imperfection's vice.

My Sweetheart.

I went to bed the other night,
　　My sleep was sweet in part;
I dreamed I saw a lovely sight,
　　It was my dear sweetheart.

She sat in the window watching,
　　As I went down the street;
I threw a kiss back to her,
　　Her face seem'd blossom sweet.

My sweetheart's image was with me,
    Whichever way I went,
It banished all temptations,
    And gave me good intent.

When the world seems full of trouble,
    When things seem to go wrong:
My sweetheart's image is with me,
    And makes me brave and strong.

I return'd by early twilight,
    And as I latched the gate;
I saw from the shaded window,
    My sweetheart still did wait.

I hastened toward the window,
    I saw my sweetheart's eyes
Sparkle with a smiling welcome,
    As the stars up in the skies.

"I'm back again, dear sweetheart,"
    I said, and stoop'd to kiss
My sweetheart's face that was lifted,
    It seem'd that all was bliss.

You all have sweethearts like this one.
    Babies, sisters and brothers;
This sweetheart gives us lots of fun,
    My sweetheart was my mother.

What do you think of my sweetheart?
I shall not go any further;
Can you blame a boy my size because
He's dead in love with mother?

———•————•———

The angel who unfetter'd St. Peter,
When bound in Jerusalem's jail;
Is no greater than the angel Lincoln
Who heeded the Negro's wail.

And never in all ages,
  Since John on Patmus wrote;
Have words been put on pages
  As great as Lincoln spoke.

Lincoln's Call.

You know 'twas eighteen sixty-one,
The civil war had just begun,
The ship of state was at the place,
To picture up the South's disgrace;
And Lincoln quickly saw the point,
Where he could knock things out of joint;
And all the sight which he had seen,
Before his mind began to gleam.
He thought of countless human slaves,
Murdered, buried without a grave;
He thought of the wicked overseer,
Whose cruelty could have no peer;
He thought of the master's snarling cry—
"That Negro's worthless, let him die."
He thought of the Southern auction block,
Where human beings sold as stock;
He thought of mother's wailing cry,
When wicked men her child would buy;
He thought how cruel they could be,

To counteract the mother's plea;
He thought how men were sold like mules,
And left their wives with wicked fools;
He thought of Christian mother's weep,
To see her child drove off like sheep;
He thought of mother's vain distress,
To have a babe sold from her breast;
And worst of all since God's creation,
He thought of that abomination—
Amalgamation of the races,
On terms that give us blushing faces;
He thought of masters who had slaves,
Whose virtue they would often crave;
And she, no matter how she feel,
To master's wicked lust must yield;
These sights as dark as dark midnight,
Made angels shudder in their flight;
The goddess of the angry deep,
These horrors made her conscience weep;
The gladiator drop'd his sword,
At sight of Southern festive boards.
Diana said with heart aglow,
Such sights have never reign'd before;
These things weighed Lincoln's heart with
　　　grief,
And when the nation made him chief—

He gave a long, tremendous call,
From out the nation's senate hall,
And all the North heard his appeal,
And marched out on the battle field;
The Pilgrim Fathers, dead and gone,
Pushed brave New England in the throng,
Good William Penn said from his grave:
" My Quakers join the Lincoln wave."
The father of the country said—
" March on, it is the rightful tread!"
The heroes of Thermopylæ
Heard Lincoln's call for liberty,
And cried from out their distant graves,
"If you must die, men's freedom save."
Crispus Attucks, whose blood ran down,
When Washington was in renown,
His blood cried out "if you'd be free,
All strike at once for liberty!"
Sojourner Truth, her voice was heard,
"March on!" was the commanding word,
Nat Turner screamed out from the sod;
" I would thou precious, allwise God,
Had spared my life upon the land
To follow Lincoln's brave command,
Then I could quickly do my part,
For poor down-trodden, human hearts,

I'd help to strike that mighty blow,
To let my bondaged people go!"
John Brown's bleeding body cried:
"This is the cause for which I died!"
Frederick Douglass, grand old man,
Who aided John Brown in his plans,
Who stood with Lincoln and conversed,
Was ready now to stand the worst.
He used his voice, his pen, his mind,
And men who heard him fell in line.
These voices echoed Lincoln's sound.
And stirred the people all around;
From Maine to California's coast,
Rose freedom's great advancing host.
Men speaking in the senate hall,
Responded to the noble call;
The Gov'nors left the state affairs,
The writer left his easy chair,
The lawyer quit the city bar,
And left his office door ajar;
The bus'ness man went out his store,
Perhaps to enter there no more;
The teacher left his tutorship,
And gave his gun a lasting grip.
The student left his study desk,
And marched with teacher breast abreast,

The hunter left the stag at bay,
For Lincoln's call he must obey;
"The plow was in the furrow staid,
The herds without a keeper stray'd,"
The fish'man left his pole and line,
The blacksmith drop'd his red hot iron,
The artist let go paint and brush,
And to the army made a rush.
Husbands kissed their wives good-bye,
Left the children, went to die;
Mothers told sons to heroes be,
In the cause of liberty;
The young man in the prime of life,
Left his newly wedded wife;
The lover left his loved one's side
Whom he had vowed to make his bride,
He loved his girl with all his heart,
But country's love was now his part;
Each son and father rushed to arms,
At Lincoln's signals of alarm.
The war began, brave Lincoln stood,
As pilot in the human flood;
Again he made a long appeal,
More men were needed in the field.
His voice was heard all o'er the land,
A million men obeyed command.

At Gettysburg, brave Lincoln stood,
And he was in a better mood;
He saw the cause for which he fought,
Was plain before the people brought;
And on that bloody battlefield,
The enemies began to yield;
And Lincoln, with his God push'd pen,
Wrote these words on the hearts of men:
"All human beings claimed as slaves—
Are placed upon great freedom's wave."
And angels echoed around the throne;
"Rejoice thy freedom is thy own!"
The Negro left his master's farm,
For he had heard the last alarm,
But half in doubt and half in stress,
He wondered which would be the best—
"*If massa ketch me gwine away,*
He'll kill dis nigger shur as day;
But whats de use to stay back herr,
He's killing niggers ebry yerr,
Boss Lincoln says dat I am free,
I'll strike a blow for liberty!"
He marched out like a soldier man,
And joined the host of freedom's van.

The war moved on for two more years,
And brave men fought without a fear,

Till Sherman's host had reached the sea,
And Grant had captured noble Lee,
Then men laid down their arms of yore,
And peace did reign from shore to shore,
Now Lincoln's work was bravely done,
The confidence of Men he'd won,
His enemies he'd conquered well,
And they before him prostrate fell.
He'd kept the faith, he'd fought his fight,
And in the stillness of the night—
When he least look'd for any strife,
A demon struck him for his life.
He fell a corpse to mortal man,
In this down trodden, sinful land;
His soul had heard the angel's cry;
"Thy work's complete, thy home's on
     high,"
So when the general roll is called,
Including, Wickliffe, Luther, Paul;
Men who have died to set men free,
Lincoln's name on the list will be.
And men who dwell upon the earth,
Will yet concede to Lincoln's worth,
And burn his birthday in the minds,
Of children 'till the end of time.
As long as there remains a trace

Of Afric blood in mortal face,
So long will Lincoln honored be,
His virtues sung from sea to sea.

Hurrah for McKinley!

Hurrah for McKinley!
　　Hurrah for Hobart!
And the St. Louis convention
　　That didn't mind revolts,
We have rallied round the flag boys,
　　Rallied once again,
Hear the cry of freedom and McKinley.

Hurrah for New England!
　　Hurrah for Illinois!
New York, Pennsylvania,
　　And all the other boys
Who have rallied, etc.

Hurrah for sound money!
　　Hurrah for protection—
That sends free silver
　　Where there'll be no resurrection,
We will rally, etc.

Hurrah for the nation!
   How it rings from sea to sea,
That McKinley is elected
   Which insures prosperity.
We have rallied, etc.

Hurrah! how McKinley
   Broke the Mason-Dixon line,
Boys, the solid South is broken,
   And shall be till end of time.
We have rallied, etc.

Hurrah for McKinley!
   Who's in Abe Lincoln's track,
Who believed that a gentleman,
   Can be either white or black.
Let us rally, etc.

Hurrah for McKinley!
   Who called upon his state,
To help keep a Negro
   From the dreadful lynching fate.
Negroes rally, etc.

Hurrah for McKinley!
   Who said he'd have no wine,
And those at the inaugural
   To drink had to decline,
Temperance rally, etc.

The Call All Must Obey.

A voice whispered to an infant,
Sitting on its mother's knees,
"Leave that place for a moment,
I want you to go with me,"
"How can I leave my mamma's lap,
And do without her sweet smiles,
How can I live without her aid?"
Replied the innocent child.

The same voice whispered to a child,
Who knew not the right from wrong,
"Come child, leave your play for awhile,
And join this mighty throng,"
The child replied in earnest tones,
"I cannot go with you now—
You see what I have here to do,
My play house is all torn down."

"Come," said the stern voice to a youth,
While plodding along his way,
And many youths were with him there,
All cheerful and full of play.
"How can I come," replied the youth,
"I'm hastening on to school,
And if I'm late," my mother says,
"Its against the teacher's rule."

"Come," the voice said to a maid,
Just in her twentieth year,
While men were passing too and fro,
Some in hope and some in fear;
"How can I come," replied the maid,
"While all of life's temptations
Surround my head, and I must be
A factor to the nation."

The voice approached a bright young man
Just entering the prime of life,
"Come," said the voice, the young man
        stopped,
As if in a human strife.
"How can I come? My days are brief,
The responsibility
That rests upon my shoulders,
Is spread from sea to sea."

The voice then sought a poet's abode,
Who was seeking after a rhyme,
And the poet had an answer
Both elusive and sublime.
"How can you ask for me to come,
Leave me to myself I pray,
For the verse which I am writing
The hearts of men will sway."

"Come," said the voice to a songster
As she raised her alto voice,
And the music sent forth by her,
Made the hearts of men rejoice.
"How can I come," said the songster,
"This world is sinking in sin,
And I am to sing God's mercies
Into the hearts of men."

"Come," said the voice to a statesman,
While speaking in the senate hall,
And his voice aroused the senate
Like troops at a bugle call.
"How can I come," said the statesman,
While our dear ship of state,
Is hanging, trembling, weakening,
At the sight of future fate?"

"Come," said the voice to a mother,
With her children at her side,
And she made the home a haven,
For her husband to abide.
"Oh, I can't come," the mother said,
"I pray you let me stay,
For how can I leave my darlings
To wander from me astray?"

The voice sent out no more appeals,
The baby left its mother,
The child with a torn down play house
Didn't stop to build another;
The youth, returning home from school,
Responded to the call,
And the maiden with her beauty
Had to enter in the thrall.

And the young man meditated,
For he was just in his prime,
But he joined the great procession
When the voice called, it was time;
And the poet, with his meekness,
Had to quit his composition;
For the voice had called him hither,
It was due a recognition.

The songster's voice was heard no more,
The world still had its sins,
The statesman left the senate floor,
And was heard no more by men;
And the mother left her children,
And they cried with sobbing breath.
But the voice which spoke—men must
    obey,
It was the voice of death.

Harriet Beecher Stowe's Works.
"Uncle Tom's Cabin."

That grand and noble woman dear,
  Called Harriet Beecher Stowe,
The book she wrote without a fear
  Drove slavery from our shore.
To know her works, to feel her worth,
  Go read that noble book
And see what dauntless words she wrote,
  What fearful risks she took.

It struck a blow to slavery's tree,
  That burned its very life;
It scorched the undergrowth around,
  And left it in a strife;
It parched the branches to a crisp,
  Withered the leaves in twain,
It drove the sap into the ground
  To never rise again.

Dark slavery rested on the base,
  That Africans were brutes,
That they should be a white man's slave
  Or dwell in destitute;
It said his sensibility
  Was not of human kind,
And if he loved, 'twas not the love
  Which with the heart combines.

And hence the children could be sold,
    Husband and wife untied,
And with a mind all full of glee,
    In distant parts abide;
No matter what the master did
    To slaves who were akin,
'Twas just the same as with a mule,
    The master didn't sin.

These doctrines were supported by
    Religion, law and science,
The preacher who preached otherwise,
    Was held up in defiance;   ·
The surgeon taught that Negro flesh
    Under the whip and knife,
Was not affected like white men,
    Hence 'twas not human strife.

Politicians said that it was
    Fixed as the lasting hills,
And God considered it as pure
    As nature's rippling rills;
The statesman, judge and governor
    Said that it was a rule,
The Negro slave should have the same
    As oxen, horse and mule.

5

Men divine, wrote book upon book,
　　Forcing restitution,
And tried to prove that slavery was
　　A God sent institution.
To speak, to write, to think against
　　This inhumanity,
Was nothing but a case of what
　　Was called insanity.

It was at such a time as this
　　That Harriet Beecher Stowe,
Called "Uncle Tom" upon the scene,
　　And made him walk before
The gaze of all the countries 'round,
　　She made him speak and cry,
In twenty diff'rent languages
　　She made him pray and sigh.

She then asked all the world who heard
　　His wild distressing prayer,
If 'twas not likely that a heart
　　Humane is stationed there;
She brought forth George and showed his
　　grand
　　Affections for his wife,
His love for liberty, and how
　　He fought the slavish strife.

She brought Haley, the Negro trader,
   Who had no human heart,
Who stole the virtue of his slaves,
   And then the lash impart;
Who took a newly wedded wife
   Before her husband's gaze,
Could the devil have seen all this,
   · He would have stood amazed.

She then showed forth the Christian heart
   Of Mister Shelby's wife,
Who sympathized with all the slaves
   In their discouraged strife;
Who wept when she first heard the news
   From her dear husband bold,
When she asked where was Uncle Tom,
   He said " the brute is sold."

These things and hundreds, thousands more,
   This noble book had shown,
And there stood Harriet Beecher Stowe,
   Between pulpit and throne;
She stood nearer the Throne of God,
   Than all false priests before,
And turned the search light on to show
   The heartache and the woe.

She wrote brave words and spead them,
    Upon the human breeze,
That made pro-slav'ry clergymen,
    Draw in their breath and sneeze;
Her shafts were sent hilt deep into
    The tender, human heart,
Just like the shepherd boy who smote
    The giant with his dart.

This book had made the world grow mad,
    With slavery and its crime,
Before the bloody battlefield,
    With marching tread did chime;
Before John Brown had died to save,
    . Before great Lincoln's call,
Before brave Sherman reached the sea,
    Before Grant captured all.

She called from out its slumb'ring tomb,
    Affections of the soul,
She armed them with eternal light,
    And sent them forth so bold
Against the greed, the gain, the lust,
    That these two forces fought,
Like Wolfe and Montcalm on the plain,
    Till right had error wrought.

Harriet Beecher Stowe's Monument.

She has builded a human monument
    The walls of which will stand,
Long after she's departed from
    The dwellers in the land,
Long after buildings have crumbled,
    · That are planted on the sand.

She decided to build for others,
    And the building sheltered her not,
And some who dwell within there,
    Through all time shall know her not,
And beneath the roof of the building
    She'll have no lot or part.

And yet when the days shall have ended,
    And beneath the roof tree's shade,
The children and grand children,
    . In childish ways have played,
And passed from under the building,
    And vanished into the shade;

Some dweller beneath the building,
    Thinking of when it was new,
May say as his heart turns backward,
    Keeping his age in view,
The woman who built this building,
    Builded better than she knew.

And she, though she has passed onward,
   Hearing the Master's call,
May say, though it may not matter
   To her what the building befall,
That it's better to build for others,
   Than to have no building at all.

Sonnet, October.

Here in sweet Nature's lonely gale,
   The leaves are gone;
The autumnal woods, all 'round our vale,
   Have glory on.

I roam these woods that nature crowns
   With splendor's glow;
Where the company of trees look down
   On fields below.

This month is the gloomiest and saddest
   Of all the year;
For in it nature's summer gladness
   All disappear.

Nature all around serene elates
   Us from the sod;
And points the heart and mind of man,
   Towards the throne of God.

Maceo—Cuba's Liberator.

While Washington at Valley Forge,
   Endured the winter's pest;
And while he was taking Yorktown
   Dear Cuba was oppressed.

When England tried the second time,
  To rule this country great;
Brave Cuba, although in her prime,
  Had not a ship of state.

When Winfield Scott took Mexico,
  And captured Vera Cruz,
Brave Cuba and young Maceo
  Were punished and abused.

When John Brown died that we might
    live,
  When Lincoln called for men;
Brave Cuba was surrounded with
  The untold Spanish sins.

When Grant and Meade fought for dear
    life,
  When Lincoln said "you're free,"
Brave Cuba, under Spanish strife,
    Said "give me liberty?"

Thus time moved on, God was invoked,
  And year succeeded year;
Brave Cuba fought—sometime with
    hope,
  And sometime full of fear.

But God who's always here with men,
   Had Him a man in store;
And at the heights of Spanish sins,
   He called forth Maceo.

When Maceo with courage strong
   Took charge of battle fields;
Like withered leaves in wintry storms,
   The enemies did yield.

He gave this dauntless, brave command,
   " We must have liberty—
And in the name of God and man,
   Our Cuba must be free!"

At this appeal the Island shook,
   The natives said they would;
And Maceo with anxious looks,
   As firm as fossils stood.

The natives all were 'lectrified,
   At sight of Maceo's form;
And they would stand and do or die,
   At Maceo's alarm.

The Spaniards, anxious to succeed,
   Discarded warring rules;
Resorted to the foulest deeds,
   Of all the crim'nal schools.

They used man's wicked, cunning ways,
    They gave him friend's salute;
They falsified to ambush him,
    They took his life like brutes.

But e'er he died he told his men,
    That Cuba must be free;
The death he died has given them
    The price of liberty.

Arnold became his country's foe,
    Judas betrayed his Christ;
The Spaniards entrapped Maceo
    At manhood's sacrifice.

They crucified the Son of man,
    His cause still moves the world;
They burned John Huss and yet he stands,
    Before us as a pearl.

They killed good Abr'am Lincoln,
    The cause for which he died
Still moves the world, still cheers men's
        hearts,
    With men he still abides.

They killed the noble Maceo,
    The world's in sympathy;
It says that foul act implores
    That Cuba must be free.

The God of Israel's Maceo,
Of Lincoln's liberty,
Has written "let my people go,"
Dear Cuba shall be free.

Dear Cuba, for a host of years,
"Queen of the Antilles,"
Thy Maceo without a fear,
Has died to set thee free.

Y. M. C. A. Founder.
Sir Geo. Williams.

Sir George Williams, noble man,
Half 'cent'ry 've passed away,
Since thou first didst raise thy hand
To start the Y. M. C. A.

One little room marked the spot,
A few common chairs therein;
And now all o'er the universe,
Its sifting the souls of men.

A few young men, only a few,
Paid any heed to thee,
Today thou'rt heard in all the lands,
Thou'rt spread from sea to sea.

I think how many a thousand,
Of reckless, wayward men,
Have caught the inspiration,
And moved off from their sins.

I think of countless mothers,
Whose hearts have leaped with joy,
Because this, thy noble work,
Has saved their reckless boy.

I think of unborn millions,
Who yet must take the stage,
Who, only through this noble work
Can face the future age.

"Forever and forever,
As long as life has woes,"
Thy name shall be re-echoed
On time's terrestrial shores.

If only I might see thee,
To gaze upon thy face,
To grasp thy hand, to hear thee speak,
Then I could be embraced.

I think I could go forward,
With brave and joyful heart,
Though every step should pierce me,
With untold fiery dart.

But I must be contented,
With thy likeness and thy name,
For countless millions now rejoice,
Upon thy spreading fame.

And I am left to wonder, such
That I may stretch my hand,
To some still wearier traveler
In this same shadow land.

I gaze upon thy likeness,
As young men's earthly sage,
Thy work is old and thriving,
But thou show'st not thy age.

Dear sir, thou art not old,
Though half a century now,
May write its ragged wrinkles,
Up and down thy brow.

And even sorrow may with
A shroud thy heart enfold,
Thou art not now, and no,
Thou never will be old.

Best Thing in the World.

What is the best thing in the world?
This question to a crowd was hurled.

A preacher said "that grand old Book
Which beats all men e'er undertook."

The monk, he said, "the best of all,
Is time alone within my walls."

The sage, he whispered in a chime,
"The best is the right use of time."

The fool and idler both did sing,
"Pleasure is the best of things."

Then the soldier cried aloud, "fame,"
Spoke the statesman, "mine is the same."

Then a maid told her selection,
"Why of course its my complexion."

Said a young man, "there are two things,
A woman's beauty, and how she sings."

A mother, playing with some curls,
Said that "the best thing in the world;

Is this darling here in my arms,
Which we and angels hold as charms."

Then the wee baby gave its choice,
And it seemed like an angel's voice;

"The bes ting dat eber was or is,
Is when my mama dives me a tiss."

Conscience whispers and this is heard,
" Kindness, kindness, that is the word."

———————

From Degradation Through
Supplication to Education.
The Negro.

I was once far from civilization,
As vile as a Negro could be;
I wondered if all the creation,
Could save a poor Negro like me.

I wandered on in the darkness,
Not a ray of light could I see;
And it filled my heart with sadness,
No hope for a Negro like me.

But by the wondrous work of God,
The world's second Moses came;
And through the sea of civil strife,
Brought liberty instead of shame.

From then I started out in life,
To make a race pride mark;
But prejudice from my enemies,
Kept holding me in the dark.

And yet within that self same race,
There are some valiant men;
Who gave both their time and means,
To remove this dreadful sin.

My enemies both reared and kicked,
I could only wait and trust;
But good men defended my cause,
Like Doctors Hartzell and Rust.

"Shall the Negro be educated?"
Is being discussed by some;
But while they are discussing,
The good work's being done.

No longer in darkness I wander,
Education is shining on me;
And unto my brothers I'm trying,
To give an education free.

Dear Lord, I'll e'er give thanks to Thee,
For Thy unspeakable gift,
In bringing me out of darkness,
And allowing a chance to lift.

And with my thanks I ask Thy aid,
For those in degradation,
That they may share e'en with me,
In Christian education.

The Model Girl.

To S——

A model girl, pure from her birth,
No one can estimate her worth,
And on this dark and sinful earth—
    She's needed.

She goes to church and Sunday school,
The Bible is her vestibule,
And fam'ly prayers, her mother's rule—
    She loves them.

She always tries to do the right,
And if you try to blur and blight,
She'll hit you with the Christian light—
    She's candid.

Sometimes, before she thinks, she speaks,
You know in this a woman's weak,
But if you will explain the freak—
    She'll listen.

And if she sees immoral trash,
She treats it very cool and rash,
And all her soul seems in a flash—
    She shuns it.

C

She knows the evils of the land,
She knows the wicked ways of man,
She takes a high and lofty stand—-
　　She dreads them.

She knows if woman stands aloft,
The wicked men will scorn and scoff,
And yet when they desire betroth—
　　She charms them.

She knows that if she mingles low,
The evil class will treat her so,
And those who try to upward soar—
　　Will shun her.

She's never wrecked herself at all,
At these low dissipating balls
Where women dance and virtue falls—
　　She scorns them.

She never goes in public places,
Where men and women's evil faces
Are ever looking for disgraces—
　　She fears them.

She never strolls the streets alone,
Whene'er the sun has ceased to roam
And all the stars so brightly shone—
　　She waives it.

When men put on an outside show,
To see if woman won't adore,
While to virtue his heart's a foe—
    She's vex-ed.

She gives pleasure a reverent touch,
She never tries to know too much
Of foolishness, gab and all such—
    She's seen these.

Pure literature attracts her eyes,
Trash novels she detests, despise,
She sees the future, hears its cries—
    "Protect us!"

She knows contentment is decay,
That discontent brings brighter days
By men and women's thriving ways—
    She's busy.

She knows that early fragrance flees,
The deepest cup hath still its lees,
And she thinks there's a "yet to be"—
    She's hopeful.

She sometimes walks in slip'ry places,
But pride with all its charming graces,
Makes all the evil-minded faces—
    Respect her.

Sometimes her mind is fluctuation,
Sometimes her soul is detestation,
Sometimes her heart is admiration—
    She usurps.

You see her as she skips along,
She has not thought of any wrong,
She's firm for right, well tried and strong—
    She's dauntless.

She never has that vain belief
That someone's watching her as chief
And asking every one in brief—
    "Who is she?"

There's a secret she calls her own,
A myst'ry to most young girls unknown,
And 'gainst the outside worldly tone—
    It cheers her.

She knows the rock once cleft for all,
She stands where'er its shadows fall,
And when she leans upon its walls—
    She's strengthened.

It makes the blessed Savior smile
To see a trusty, faithful child
Go through the world pure, undefiled--
    She knows it.

The eye may try to be a charm,
But from the heart's imperial throng,
Come penciled lines of right and wrong—
    She's cautious.

Time's etching gives her tone of thought,
God's etching shows divinely bought
Soul stenciled by the spirit taught—
    She's fix-ed.

Her sisters all should imitate,
Her brothers should appreciate,
Her father should reconsecrate—
    And mother.

I hope her Christian spirit bold
Will dwell where summer seasons roll,
And cheerful hearts will ne'er grow old—
    She'll like it.

And when time's clouds have all gone by,
And she has quit the world of sighs,
I hope the place beyond the skies—
    Will take her.

Now some of you who read these lines,
May try to form within your minds,
The reason why I write this rhyme—
    I like her.

Well I guess that it must be true,
And if you knew her as I do,
I think you'd kinder like her too—
    She earns it.

      *   *   *   *

Oh, somewhere in this shadowed land,
A host of shining angels stand;
Somewhere the sun is shining bright,
And hearts are made of burdens, light;
Somewhere the little children shout
And walk the streets, their hearts are stout;
Somewhere the evil hearts of men
That tempt the little ones to sin
Are counted as a wicked shame,
And wicked men will be refrained—
From doing evil, dirty work,
Which, from the young ones, virtue jerk;
Somewhere good people congregate
And leave off those who dissipate
And make them have a strong desire
To quit their ways and come up higher;
Somewhere young men appreciate
The girl who shuns all future fates;
Somewhere good deeds are recognized,
And virtue counted as a prize;

Somewhere the angels hover 'round
To dedicate the earthly town
Because it tries to do the right
And keep the Lord's will e'er in sight;
Oh, somewhere there's security
To live a life of purity,—
　　　Not our town.

Love's Labor Lost.

Sweetheart, you know what true love is,
You know we have loved each other,
You know that we have sometimes felt
As near as sister and brother.

You know, my dear, the time has been
When to be in each other's sight
And to talk, and hear each other talk
To both our hearts was delight.

You know it has not been so long
Since we, in saying good night
Would fondly hug and kiss each other,
Oh my! what a change tonight!

Can it be true that some one else
Has entered into your heart,
And tells me that from this time on
I shall have no lot or part?

Can it be true that all my love,
Of which I so proudly boast,
Is drift-wood on the restless sea
And my task, "Love's labor lost?"

Deception.

Well, dearest one, I hope my heart
Will stop its bitter sigh,
Because it never more can share
Thy glorious destiny;
My love has never sought reward,
'Twas joy enough for me
To dwell alone at certain times
And cherish thoughts of thee.

My mother to her child once gave
Affection's untold wealth,
Since then I've seen the swift decay
Of hope, and joy, and health;
I murmured not, at heaven's decree,
Though thus of all bereft,
When you and I began to love
A world of bliss was left.

Though other ties thy heart now bind
While we but drift apart,
Yet, am I sinning if I hide
Thine image in my heart?
So sweet, so holy was the spell
By love around me cast
That I am blinded to all love
Since this, my charm, has past.

I feel that you another love,
Yet there's a heavy trace,
And all the love of others
Those bright tints can't efface.
I hope his lot a joyous one
If you his fate control,
I'll try to seek a higher fate—
The union of the soul.

The time was, when I looked on thee
As God sent future bride,
And had a longing in my heart
To thus be satisfied;
But it is best for you and I
If we are not to wed,
To know before we go too far
Upon the lover's tread.

Farewell, beloved one, when thy brow
The cupid crown shall bind,
And when, somewhere in life's abode
You and someone combine,
Then think of one who looked on thee
With more than human pride,
And glories in the thought that you
Are someone's rightful bride.

Love Regained.

If it is really true that I have grieved thee,
You whom my soul has always loved the best,
Can you not come to me once more forgiving,
And lay your head again upon my breast?

Last night when I in grief and sorrow left you,
And heard the rapid slam of your screen door;
I felt that I toward my doom was going,
And love and joy would be mine nevermore.

The thought that caused my heart to bleed
        most freely:
I've always tried to go the true love's route,
And then to think my only heart's affection,
Myself and word did disbelieve and doubt.

And then I felt that all my earthly efforts,
Were wasted—and what we call human life,
Was nothing but a sea of disappointment,
Of myth and pain, of sorrow, grief and strife.

But since I have received from you a letter,
Which says that you have called me back
 again,
A heavy mist has gathered up before me,
When it is gone I hope there'll be no pain.

If I had known how sadly I should grieve you,
If I had thought that it was the last,
There's nothing in the world had made me
 leave you,
And now, dear heart, I hope the gloom is past.

Can you not see how I have missed you, dear-
 est,
How I regret I ever gave you pain;
How heretofore I held you first and nearest,
O love, may I say you are mine again?

I will be kinder to you. I was fretful;
Life had so much that was too hard to bear,
I did not understand how self-forgetful,
Your love had lightened every pain and care.

We grow too sure of those who never give us
A single anxious thought; they are our own:
I did not dream how much I really loved you,
Until I thought my priceless treasure gone.

I hate to think of sorrow's painful palace,
I could not stand to think that you were there;
I felt that you were passing, while I love you,
Beyond me, among men that you could bear.

Yet, if 'tis true that you are still my lover,
Your own pure life no mocking chance has
    known;
Can you not now sweet consolation give me,
For grief and doubt that have so bitter grown?

Can you not just for my sake once more kiss me;
And we'll forget the words that gave us pain,
They haunt me now,—and that you love and
    miss me,
May we now call our doubts true love regain-
ed?

Love and Fear Contest.

They say that in each human heart,
    There is an unseen battle-field,
'Pon which two fighting forces meet,
    And neither one consents to yield.

I don't know who those forces are,
   There's love and hatred, hope and fear,
There's laughter with his great bazaar,
   There's sorrow with its bitter tear.

Once love stepped out upon my breast,
   And gazing at the vacant skies;
Had thoughts of one it thinks the best,
   And this is what, aloud it cried:—

Just thoughts of her is music sweet,
   Dear A. V.: Oh be still my heart;
And darling with what joy it speaks,
   Oh, how it makes my senses start.

I must confess it rolls along,
   In scintillating streams of bliss;
Until it mingles with my song—
   And thrills me like a pulsing kiss.

Then fear came forth upon the scene,
   And said "beware of passive bliss;
For things are not just what they seem,"
   Then love replied in words like this:

I recognize the Christian plan,
   This earthly life is built upon;
It gives a wife to ev'ry man,
   And I'll be satisfied with one.

Yes surely I'll be satisfied,
  If I can get the one I love;
The one who's taken away my heart,
  And carries it where'er she roves.

But fear, I trembled at one thought;
  If she consents to be my bride,
What, oh what, if I can't supply
  The things to make her satisfied.

Could I be happy? No, not I,
  I'd rather be adrift at sea,
With the storms around me raging,
  And no one there to care for me.

But I will do the best I can,
  The noblest precepts to obey;
But sometimes tides of fierce desires,
  Around my heart doth surge and sway.

I must restrain the thoughts I feel,
  Now glowing in my fervent breast;
They're not conducive to my weal,
  Simply a love and fear contest.

Fixed Love.

You know that I love you, yet bid me adieu,
Can happiness live when absent from you?
Will sleep on my eyelids e'er sweetly alight
When greeted no more by a tender good night?

Oh, never, for deep is the record enshrined,
Thy look' and thy voice will survive in my mind;
Though age may the treasure of memory remove
Unshaken shall flourish the thought that I love.

Through life's winding valley, in anguish, in rest,
Exalted in joy, or by sorrow depressed;
Just place in the mirror that lies on my heart
Thine image shall never one moment depart.

When time, life, and all that we mortals hold
    dear,
Like visions, like dreams, shall at last disap-
    pear,
Though raised among seraphs to realms above,
Unshaken shall flourish the thought that I love.

New Year's Greeting.

To a loved one.

As this is the first of the year,
    And I am all alone,
I thought I'd try to draw me near
    To thee, my dear, my own.

Yes, I'm alone, and don't you know
    I do not like to speak,
Yet I will, as 'tis fitting now,
    My wanted silence break.

There is a love that in my soul
    Burns silent and alone;
It kindles flames around my heart,
    You know that heart's your own.

The dearest idol I have known
    Is my dear Lord above;
The next one which I long to own
    Is you, my precious love.

I call myself both chaste and pure,
    And free from passions low;
Hence I know what I say is true,
    For conscience speaketh so.

Thy Christian spirit I do prize,
    For this I've surely seen;
For this thou'rt precious to my eyes
    As gold and jewels sheen.

Thy sweet face I esteem indeed,
    So modest and so kind;
Its presence I forever need,
    May I call that face mine?

I've never written such a poem
    To mortal girl before,
Because I've never loved a woman
    As the one I now adore.

During the year that's past and gone,
  I've launched in a new field;
That tender chord broke with a song,
  And now to love I yield.

As I review my past year's work,
  Some things I've left undone;
And yet I feel that I have gained,
  If your confidence I've won.

I hope that I have not done that
  To bring thee any pain;
For all I've done was done in love,
  Dear, is my love in vain?

Throughout the year of ninety—
  If lovers still we be;
Let's have that love that warms both
    hearts
  And let our minds be free.

Miss Snow Flake and the Lovers.

Little Miss Snow Flake came to town
  All dressed up in a velvet gown;
And nobody looked so fresh and fair
  As little Miss Snow Flake, I declare.

7

Out of the cozy cloud she stepped,
   Where most all of the snowflakes slept;
She thought her beauty would ne'er be known
   If in a crowd, so she came alone.

All alone from the great blue sky
   Where the swift clouds went scudding by,
All the way from the bright abode
   Down somewhere near the city road.

There she rested near out of breath,
   And there she speed'ly met her death;
And nobody could exactly tell
   Just where little Miss Snow Flake fell.

But a very prominent young man,
   Both for love and his heart's command
Was out that night to see his girl,
   When the Miss Snow Flake gave her twirl.

So when the young man said he'd go,
   He op'd the door and cried out "O!"
And he fell back most out of breath
   And almost scared his girl to death.

That Miss Snow Flake of whom we speak,
   Had struck the young man on the cheek;
His shoes were of the patent kind,
   His overcoat he'd left behind.

And she says: "What's the matter dear?"
  He says, "See how it snows out here,"
And if I have to go out doors,
  I'll get frost bitten on the nose."

These two did love from depth of heart;
  In danger's realm they could not part;
And now I ask both men and maids,
  Whether this man went home or stayed.

The Trip I Would Like to Take.

Man has a curious appetite,
  He's all the time wishing to go;
And if he had the wings of a kite,
  He'd travel this wide world o'er.

Sometime I'd like to go away,
  Far over the Rocky Mountains;
Where the rainbows dance on silvery
      rays,
Of California's fountain.

In the rocks below, in the trees above,
  In the brooklet and the river
I could read and know that God is love,
  And of all good things the giver.

I would like to go to the Yellowstone,
And witness the giant geysers;
To see its grandure there alone,
Would surely make me wiser.

For in the roar the hissing stream,
As it issues from the crater;
I could there learn more of the bound-
    less theme,
Of a kind and wise Creator.

Then I would go to the great Black Hills,
Across the plains of Dakota;
And take a stroll to the rippling rills,
And lakes of Minnesota.

I would sit on lake Itaska's shore
Where the Mississippi rises;
And Minnehaha's laughing roar
Would fill me with glad surprises.

I'd go to the "Dreamy city,"
Well yes, and while I was there;
I'd make myself a committee,
To witness the ruins of the fair.

I would journey then to Southern climes,
'Mid Florida's blooming bowers;
There to see God's work sublime,
In the beautiful, fragrant flowers.

From there I'd make a flying trip,
To the gateway city of the east;
And from its great exhibits,
And Negro arts I'd feast.

And then a little cruise I'd take,
Along the Atlantic Ocean;
To where the earth with a powerful quake
Put Charleston in wild commotion.

I would still continue on my way,
Through the Shenandoah valley,
Where the " boys in blue and the boys
    in gray,"
Would waver again to rally.

Then I'd go to Niagara's Falls,
And there I would learn and wonder,
For God can teach in a voice that calls
From the cataract's deafening thunder.

I'd wander over into Texas,
To visit a loving sister,
I'd talk of the days gone and past,
And tell her how I had missed her.

I would then cross into Mexico,
And visit those ancient mounds;
That were built hundreds of years ago,
Whose mystery man has not found.

I'd go to Italy's sunny climes,
To the "city of seven hills,"
And from its structure of ancient times,
And grandure I'd be filled.

I'd go to the unspeakable Turk,
Among the Armenian strife;
And ask them how from conscience
    clear,
They still took human life.

I'd go before the courts of France,
Where Waller was in jail;
I'd prick their ears with facts, and make
Their conscience go his bail.

Then I would journey to the North,
To see that Shakespearian land;
Where Hamlet said from conscious wrath
"What a piece of work is man."

I would then go to the Holy Land,
Where the Saviour was crucified,
Then I could better keep His commands,
Seeing the place where He died.

I'd traverse all the paths of Paul,
Among the various nations;
Then I'd go where man had his fall,
And view the land of creation.

I'd then go into Egypt land,
Where Joseph was sent by God,
I'd stand where Moses gave command,
I'd tread where Israel trod.

I'd go into Africa's Jungles.
Where the Bible has never been,
And attempt God's word to mumble,
In the hearts of heathen men.

I'd visit then the Isles of the sea,
And view those novel scenes,
I'd tell the people what to be,
And not what they should seem.

If I was able Christian friends,
To travel this journey through,
It would not be for sights or scenes,
But teaching men to be true.

And if I could on this journey roam,
My trip would not be ended;
I'd like to view the eternal home,
And there be recommended.

Alone with Jesus.

Over the hills and dales, Jesus, that I strolled
　　　in the long ago,
I am wandering once again my Lord, where
　　dame nature's teachings glow;
And I pause by the way to whisper, Lord, to
　　the blossoms sweet and fair,
A poor little faded sorrow, Lord, there's no-
　　body else to care.

Springtime with all its joys, Jesus, is out on
　　the old highway,
But the breezes sigh as they pass me by and
　　over the meadows stray;
Mournfully sigh the breezes, Lord, as they
　　pass me standing there,
By the pine tree row where the daises grow,
　　and nobody for me cares.

Standing alone with the trees, my Lord, I am
　　lost in a pensive dream,
I am floating away through the happy day,
　　when my youthful conscience gleam,
The conscience that shared my love for you,
　　The conscience that smiled as fair,
As the promise true I was glad to view, with
　　nobody else to care.

Over the hills and dales, Jesus, in the shadowing cool of day,
Comes the echo low of long ago the tenderest things to say.
And I smile anew as the twilight comes to banish my long despair
With a thought of You that is sweet and pure and wonder if You will care.

Something speaks to me, Jesus, the breezes are singing low,
Something that thrills the conscience, Lord, and gives them a brighter glow;
Something that soothes the pinching pain I have patiently learned to wear,
Through the endless day on the sweet highway, it seems, Lord, that you are there.

Then Jesus said "I'm with you now, and will be with you always,
We'll go together and make things better along the sweet highway,"
We strolled through the meadows together, the days seemed endless fair,
He told me of His home on high and the many mansions there.

My Bible.

From Santa Claus' most sacred nook,
Came forth this little prayerful book,
   On Christmas day.

As the old year is past and gone,
And the new year begins with song,
   I'll read its ray.

As we look back o'er our past lives,
And see from whence blessings derived,
   We all should pray.

Oh! who so brave with earthly care,
As not to give an humble prayer,
   Some part of day?

What heart so clear, so pure within,
That needeth not some check from sin,
   Needs not to pray?

Mid each day's anger, what retreats,
More needful than the mercy seat,
   On that last day?

What thoughts more dear than that our
   God, His face should hide
And say through life's swelling tide,
   No time to hear?

You have launched your boat on life's gid-
 · dy sea,
And your all is afloat for eternity,
    When you have no time to pray.

You have chosen the world, with its mis-
    named pleasures;
You have chosen the world before heav-
    en's own treasures,
    If you have no time to pray.

When the stars are concealed, the rudder
    gone,
Heaven will be sealed to the wandering
    one,
    Who has no time to pray.

The grave shall yield its prize when from
    the wondering skies,
Christ shall with wondering angels come,
    to wake those sleeping in the tomb,
    Then you'll have no time to pray.

Oh! may it ever be said, that this book,
    by us, shall be read,
And, may we all together meet, Embrac-
    ing the Redeemer's feet,
    For we have time to pray.

Fashion.

Master of the woman's kingdom,
    What is this men say of thee?
Thou art what the woman honors,
    Thou art all some care to be!

And they say, you're loved by many,
    Loved too often, loved too well,
Just as if there could be any
    Over loving in thy swell.

Sir, no doubt these dear good people,
    Were you not their earthly God,
Could build them a Christian steeple
    Up to heaven, without a hod.

You and Solomon the wise man,
    Are two fellows of a kind,
Just to please the wants of woman,
    You would leave your soul behind.

And those sisters that can't catch you,
    What a plight they must be in!
For the song you sing oft leads them
    To commit an awful sin.

Now all wicked aspirations,
    Do not spring from souls depraved
Into fashion. Its elation
    Is the sanctity it craved.

In the world's long reign of struggles,
    Thou hast played an active part;
Hast thou during all thy journey,
    Mended up a broken heart?

Thou hast found some so despondent,
    Who the name of God despise;
Hast thou tried to once control by
    Pointing over to Paradise?

When thou findest men and women,
    Struggling for the higher life,
Dost thou lend a hand to help them?
    No, thou causest human strife!

Woman tries to be thy servant,
    Disobeys dame Nature's laws,
Ere she reaches thirty summers,
    Shattered frame and sunken jaws.

Ere she comes to age of duty,
    Her own grave she's quickly dug,
Simply 'cause thy longing beauty,
    Keeps her body in a shrug.

You go with them to the church house,
    They do not hear the preacher;
You are all their heart's elation,
    You are their Sunday teacher.

Thou hast seized the cross of Jesus,
  Loaded it with new born sins;
Overloaded it with folly,
  Placed it on His back again,

Thou, in thy domain of pleasure,
  Crush the thorns through Jesus' crown;
Making men laugh at His passions,
  And the blood that's trickling down.

Thou art in the great theatres,
  Thou art on the ball room floor;
Thou art in the gambler's dungeon,
  Thou dost all men's sorrows know.

Thou hast severed many fam'lies,
  Children off from home have strayed;
Father sits there broken hearted,
  Mother joined thy great parade.

Well, no doubt you had your troubles,
  Devils blue that fought your hopes;
But you have it back in double,
  Woman's kingdom in a lope.

If your lady love stuck by you,
  In the mediaeval day,
Ah! dear fashion, here is to you,
  In these times that is the way.

Always sure you have your glory,
  It increases and takes well;
What the end is of thy story,
  There's no paragraph to tell.

At thy feet a million people
  Lie today without a breath;
Who, in worshiping thy steeple,
  Found an everlasting death.

* * *

Strong Drink.

There is a crime upon this land,
  That works both night and day,
It gives its wicked, dark command,
  The hearts of men it sways.

It brings men from all ranks of life,
  Down to the brutish tribe,
Where everything is war and strife,
  And wickedness abide.

It goes into the sacred homes,
  Where peace and love should be;
It makes the children long to roam,
  And home affections flee.

It knocks the noble mother down,
    It kicks her on the floor,
And makes her husband give her frown,
    Which follows with a blow.

Sometimes it curses mother dear,
    And stabs her bleeding heart,
And, filled with sorrow, love, and fear,
    From husband's face departs.

It strips the children naked and
    Leaves them without their food;
It breaks the fam'ly coral strand,
    And leaves things dark and rude.

It takes the young man in his prime,
    And makes him curse his mother,
But this is the beginning crime,
    It takes him even further.

It makes him take the spotless heart
    Of some bright, prosperous maid,
And take it to the demon mart,
    And there has it arrayed.

It makes her break the marriage vow,
    While in her honey moon,
And long from his demoniac rows,
    To roam and cure her swoons.

It makes the young man poison all
  The tissues of her system,
And various diseases make
  This maid their deathly victim.

He soon vacates this world himself,
  And leaves a weeping widow,
With mind, and soul, and heart bereft,
  A past all dark and bitter.

He leaves with her an infant child,
  With an intemperate birth;
To, if it lives, go and defile
  Some other one of worth.

This demon takes a million youths
  In every passing year,
And makes them disregard the truth,
  And give to right a jeer.

It strikes a million mothers' hearts,
  That should be filled with joy,
And makes their inner senses start
  With " Where's my precious boy?"

It takes a million mid-life men,
  From out the state and church,
And takes them to its wicked den
  Where conscience walks with crutch.

It takes the old retiring sage,
    Who should give good advice,
And makes him, in his ripe old age
    Detest the living Christ.

It makes the leaders of the state
    Forget that man needs limit,
And names this crime industry great,
    Because there's money in it.

It fills our penitent'ry walls,
    It runs the county farms;
It overflows the prison stalls,
    With all its death-like charms.

Its fruits are the asylums, and
    Poor-houses, and hospitals,
The gambling hell, the illfamed house,
    Where satan plays the fiddle.

It wrecks the system of a man,
    Promotes arterial action,
Inflames the liver and it stands
    Amidst diseases' factions.

This preys upon the active lungs,
    Which paints the hectic cheek,
And prophecies a sepulcher
    For a consumptive freak.

This follows on the fatal train,
   Promoting untold sadness,
Until it strikes upon the brain,
   Which brings distressing madness.

The victim feels himself in hell
   While he's with living men;
And he could whet the dagger well,
   To take the life of friends.

His wicked passions are inflamed,
   With crime, with lust, with anger,
And drops his heart in human shame
   Beneath all human candor.

He seeks to hold relentless war,
   With God, or man, or self;
All men to him are at a par,
   His mind is all bereft.

This crime is universal,
   It travels this wide world o'er,
It makes men's hearts reversal,
   And puts conscience out the door.

It has swallowed generations,
   And made whole nations shrink;
Its mission is damnation,
   This crime is named "Strong Drink."

Sam Jones.

Who is it for the last two weeks
   Has been in our town,
And on the end of every tongue
   We hear his name resound?

Who is it every night and day,
   Would draw a mighty crowd,
And from the depth of his own heart,
   Poured forth God's truth aloud?

Who was it that appealed to all,
   To every class of men,
And showed the dreadful wickedness,
   In their indulging sins?

Who was it called the children out
   And told them what to do,
And told them what they must forbid,
   To be God's children true?

Who touched that little tender chord
   Within their youthful hearts,
And deep down in their youthful souls
   Did God's own word impart?

Who called the mothers out one day
  And opened to their view,
The way they must through life's conflicts
  Lead their dear children through?

Who told them that their mission was
  More sacred than them all,
That they built up a platform where
  The child would stand or fall?

Who told the wives that selfsame day
  What was their sacred duty,
And told the daughters, young and old,
  That character was beauty?

Who told the young men that the world
  Was hanging on its fate,
And waiting for some noble men
  To fill the church and state?

And then who told the fathers dear
  That they too had a hand,
That on the fam'ly's record book
  Were traces of their hands?

Who told them that the faithful wife,
  Who was the queen of home,
Were due all his affections, that
  He had no time to roam?

Who told them that those children dear
  Now playing at mother's knee,
Depended on their father's strength,
  They'd be what father'd be?
Who called men from the gambling hell,
  And told them that the cards,
That they had pushed from day to day
  Would their own child retard?
Who called men from the low saloons
  And told them that the cup
Would cause their sons to be like them,
  No better than a pup.
Who drew the tears to Christian eyes,
  And caused their souls to weep;
Who made some sinners cry aloud,
  "I'll try God's word to keep?"
But time is brief and I must stop,
  Do you all understand;
Excell and Steward both were there,
  But Sam Jones was the man.

A Human Artist.

Would that I were an artist
And while I stand in time
I could show our youths eternity,
While they are in their prime.

Would that I were an artist,
And to this American nation
I'd picture out the lynching crime
And show its revelation.

Would that I were an artist,
I would draw a human heart,
I'd show to men and women
The effects of corrupted parts.

And then I'd outline Paradise,
And give a celestial view,
I'd show to men their future home,
If while on earth they're true.

Maid and Mosquito.

A maiden sat at midday hour,
Beneath a shady tree,
She heard a noise within her bower,
"My soul, what can it be?"

She looked around, but looked in vain,
For nothing met her gaze,
She quieted down to read again,
Its voice again was raised.

Hark! hush! I know it can't be far,
'Tis clearer than before,
Is it the whistle of the car,
Or distant thunder's roar?

Ah! soon I'll know for here it comes,
My nerves quake in their bud,
For with its long and pointed tongue
'Twill pierce and drink my blood.

My doom is sealed, I know my fate,
O! would that I were a man,
He darts from his ærial state
And lights upon her hand.

She screamed for help and raised a stick
And fought, for she could not hide,
The great mosquito gave a kick,
Fell from her hand and died.

She could not read because she had
Deep meditating thoughts,
She stood and gazed upon the spot
Where she'nd the skeeter fought.

But presently she heard a noise
Circling around her head,
And there was a score of skeeters,
Singing songs of the dead.

She closed her book and sat upright,
The skeeters increased their mew,
She saw she could not stand it long,
So she grabbed her book and flew.

Magna est Veritas.

I want to be a soldier,
From realms of heavenly light,
Be pure in soul, and bold in heart,
And guide all mankind right.

I want to serve the weary,
And cause a light to shine
In every path that's dreary,
To cheer when strength declines.

I want that meek and tender glory
That fills the soul with life,
So dear to youth, to age and hoary,
To all so dear and free from strife.

Our lives are unincumbered
By depressing want and woe,
And the days fly by unnumbered,
Smoothly down time's path they go.

I'm trying to forge a key
To ope the gates of heaven;
That key's in the hearts of men,
And back its bolts are driven.

Lord strengthen me, that while I stand
On the rock, and strong in Thee,
I may stretch out a loving hand
To wrestle a troubled sea.

Lord, teach me, that I may teach
The things thou dost impart,
Help me and my wants to reach
The depths of many a heart.

"To place my thoughts in one line,"
In a decoration of beauty,
And get behind my conscience,
My whole life's work is duty.

These words come to my mind,
"The work of the world is done by a
    few,"
These words come from my conscience,
"God looks for a part to be done by
    you."

Just Married.

You've launched in a new vessel,
And down life's stream you're going,
Remember that life's tides will rise,
And life's winds will be blowing.

But while the storms are raging,
Stand by each other's side,
And just as 'tis when all is calm,
Your boat will stem the tide.

Eternal love and wisdom drew
The plan of earth and skies,
Let His great love be e'er your guide
Throughout your married lives.

May your lives be prosperous,
And always full of love,
And may you both be led by Him
Whose home's in heaven above.

All earthly good we wish thee,
All good for thee and thine,
And still not only earthly,
But all that is divine.

May heaven and earth both mingle,
May earth and heaven be one
All through your earthly journey,
Till set your earthly sun.

The heart that you have given,
The heart that's given to you,
May both be joined together,
May both be good and true.

In shadow and in sunshine,
In sighing and in song,
May heaven bless your union,
Throughout your whole life long.

Woman in Congress.

Well, a woman went to congress,
  Because she was elected;
She lived in a woman's era,
  Hence she was not objected.

All of the leading problems
  Of the country's weal or woe,
Were discussed while there at congress,
  And her mind was all aglow.

And a lady friend said to her;
  "Did you catch the speaker's eye?"
"I sure did, and I'll tell you
  The simple reason why!"

"I wore my navy blue bloomers,
　And heliotrope skirt waist;
And his eyes were ever on me,
　I dressed to suit his taste."

This woman was a congressman
　She had the states at heart;
Of course she had to dress that way,
　For that's a woman's part.

＊
＇
———·——·——

Life Pictures.

One little look from mother,
Has caused the innocent child,
To go into spasmodic shame
Or a distillation of smiles.

Just one little word when spoken,
In a soft and gentle tone,
May send reviving spirits
Into a heart of stone.

Sometimes a soul that's frigid,
Though frozen up for years,
May, by an act of kindness
Be melted into tears.

So we, whose lives are lighted
With all the world holds dear,
Should give to those less favored
A kindly word of cheer.

These little things we count for naught,
Hold all our greatest power,
The dewdrop on the thirsty bud
Opens the fragrant flower.

Quietude.

When my daily toil is ended
And the sun begins to wane,
O. if I could find some quietude,
To dispel my care and pain.

What a peaceful change I'd witness,
How my heart with rapture'd glow,
While the murmurs of the quietude
Lull my soul in sweet repose.

Quietude while I am busy,
Calmly on the bustling shore,
Better hearts than mine can love thee,
Purer lives thy peace adore.

Should perchance someone enjoying
Residence within thy shrine,
Bury in thy placid bosom,
All his cares along with mine.

A Christmas Gift.
(Bible.)

Do you know that this is Christmas,
    And this little book is sent
As a messenger of One who
    Came to earth with good intent?

Came to earth, left home in glory,
    On that first cold Christmas day,
And He's left this as a token,
    Showing us the right of way.

When you ponder o'er its pages,
    Think of how the Savior died,
How He suffered men's outrages,
    Loved them, yet was crucified.

Can we count redemption's treasure,
    Scan the glory of God's love?
Such shall be the boundless measure
    Of His blessings from above.

When the Christmases are over,
And the Savior comes again,
May you join the happy chorus,
And in glory be ordained.

The Negro's "America."

My country, 'tis of thee,
Sweet land of liberty,
    Would I could sing;
Its land of Pilgrim's pride
Also where lynched men died
With such upon her tide,
    Freedom can't reign.

My native country, thee
The world pronounce you free
    Thy name I love;
But when the lynchers rise
To slaughter human lives
Thou closest up thine eyes,
    Thy God's above.

Let Negroes smell the breeze,
So they can sing with ease
    Sweet freedom's song;
Let justice reign supreme,
Let men be what they seem
Break up that lyncher's screen,
    Lay down all wrong.

Our fathers' God, to Thee,
Author of liberty,
   To Thee we sing;
How can our land be bright?
Can lynching be a light?
Protect us by thy might,
   Great God our King!

Fleeting Spring.

Friends, my dear friends, do you know
   That Springtime's April is gone,
And lovely May with all its show,
   Has nature's spring coat on?

Birds, little birds, yes you know
   That it is beautiful spring;
From tree to tree, the birdies go,
   On fleeting wing!

Quaker, quaker, do you know
   That the yellow is going?
More than that do you know
   That the green is growing?

Singer of songs, do you know
   That youth is flying?
That age, at the lock of your life,
   Will soon be prying?

Lover of life, do you know
That youth's hue is going?
More than that, do you know
That the gray is showing?

----•——————•————

Time—Eternity.

The Saint's Departure.

I had a dream the other night,
I saw some strange and mystic sights
    That puzzled me;
Some things I saw resembled time,
And some resembled more sublime—
    "Eternity."

The oriental Persian scenes,
The tropics with their bright sunbeams,
    Could not compare.
And even Italy's soft'ning hills,
Pleasant dales and rippling rills,
    Would stand aglare.

I saw the sun rise in the East,
And watched to see its Western feast,
    It never set;
I wandered 'round among the throng,
To see if any soul was wronged,
    But none I met.

They all had on their bright attire,
It seem'd they never would retire
    To workman's garb;
I wondered how they could exist,
Forever in a pleasure mist,
    My senses throbb'd.

I strolled around the city's limit,
To find the tombstones that were in it,
    And as I went
I saw towers and castles high,
But not a white slab to my eye
    Said monument.

I sought to find the destitute,
And wondered why they were so mute,
    I felt for them;
I could not get a single sigh,
Nor even see a tearful eye,
    No face was grim.

I went into a chapel grand,
Its walls were gold.   I saw a man
    Stand by the door;
"There's no place for the poor I see!"
And he this answer made to me:
    "We have no poor."

I was perplexed, so I sat down,
Beneath a shade tree's springtime sound
    And this implied:
"Sir! whence come all these loving
    scenes,
This landscape to our eyes serene,
    Sir! where am I?"

And then out from among the leaves,
And from the pathway's flower wreathes,
    And 'cross the stream;
There came a thronging band of saints,
With countenance above complaints,
    Joy reigned supreme.

At first I thought I knew their voices,
Their greetings to me were the choicest,
    I made a start;
But they, arrayed in shining gold,
Appeared as strangers in the fold,
    I knew them not.

And when they saw me puzzled stand,
The mighty throng did clap their hands,
    Saying "welcome."
And all the mystery passed away,
The band cried out "you're here to stay,
    This is heaven!"

I found that time had gone its trip,
Eternity had fixed its grip
    On human hearts;
The rich and poor together stood,
Upon one solid brotherhood—
    Never to part.

And some one said from out the throng,
"Are all here who have conquered
    wrong?"
    He was a seer;
And voices from all generations,
Sent forth in loudest exclamation:
    "We are all here."

An angel cried "Time why depart?"
And Time replied with cheerful heart,
    I used to be;
But God, the maker of mankind,
Said some day I should be defined
    "Eternity."

Class Valedictorian.
To A. R.

The struggles you have made in school,
Today are crowned with honor;
You stand now in a vestibule,
That causes you to ponder.

School days and childhood days must end,
And life's tempestuous storms;
From every part are coming in,
Be firm! Be true! Be calm!

In conversation once you said
The highest human standing
Would be your goal. And you'd be led
By all your rights demanding.

No matter what the world may say,
Adopt this as an omen—
That you will go the right of way,
And make yourself a woman.

A gentle voice is calling thee,
The future calls for aid;
And those stern ones in death made free,
Tell you the price they paid.

Stand forth for God and liberty,
Stand forth for human rights;
In one strong effort, worthy thee,
Soul stenciled, be a light.

Enter the field of life to do.
Not just to work for gain;
For such mottoes make men untrue,
Narrowing the heart and brain.

Enter not in a feverish strife,
Nor in a giddying whirl,
For these dry the fountain of life,
And gulfs the soul in a swirl.

Enter not in a dull routine,
He who was meant to be king,
Thus will be made a dull machine,
Grinding down to a thing.

Your classmates have their eyes on you,
Your kindred watch your motion,
Your friends have all your acts in view,
Your ship is on the ocean.

And world-wide Christendom at large,
Stands waiting for your action;
And God, who shaped your fleeting barge,
Has with you a transaction.

Thus environed move forward brave,
Surmount all opposition,
And on this restless human wave,
Make better man's condition.

Go forth, thou leader of the class,
With brain ahead of brawn;
Strive e'er to gain the foremost place,
Let no man take thy crown.

As you move off into life's sea,
With skill to use the pen;
Be thou a messenger of peace,
A beacon light to men.

Press on, you have the class's hope,
Be brave and watch your course;
Success is on ahead and you
Shall gain the wished for shores.

Should I fail, not skilled in writing,
Best advise here to produce;
From the world's great pictures view it,
Put it to the best of use.

PART II.

Children's Corner.

Children's Corner.

" Little Children Love One Another."—Bible.

I wish that I had the power
  To dedicate this chapter,
There's not a single hour,
  My soul it don't enrapture.

          *   *   *

I wish I knew just what to say,
  To introduce this part;
Its on my mind both night and day,
  It penetrates my heart.

          *   *   *

I wish I had the children here,
  Well, then I couldn't write;
My mind would be in such a cheer,
  My heart in such a flight—
That I would not believe my eyes,
That I was not in Paradise.

Children's Kisses.
1 John, 3:7.

Sometimes we kiss for passion's sake,
  Sometimes we kiss through love;
Sometimes we kiss and make mistakes,
  Our kisses should be gloved.

We never know when lips impart,
  If it is false or true;
But if its from the children's heart,
  Just rest assured its pure.

We ne'er have thoughts unsatisfied,
  Which children's kisses bring;
No tearful eyes for hope denied,
  Nor taste of bitter things.

We ne'er have sense of fallen pride,
  No reason for resentment;
No thoughts of wicked Lethe's tide,
  The child's kiss brings contentment.

The hope of endless better things,
  The kiss of children wakes,
And stirs our hearts, till conscience sings
  And hearts with gladness break.

If all the kisses on the earth,
  Were pure as little children's,
And I could get my conscience's worth,
  My kisses would be millions.

" The Time of the Singing of Birds is Come."

Solomon's Song, 2:12.

I sought the sanctum of a bird,
  I wanted information;
I simply asked for just one word,
  To help in dedication.

Chirped the birdie, "Its an honor,
  If it is for the children;
For their holy, sacred corner,
  I'll give you half a million."

"Little sisters, little brothers,
  I've a message from above;
Told to me to tell to others,
  Its a heart brim full of love."

"While time is fresh and hope is new,
  While youth is lingering nigh,
Keep noble things within thy view,
  Look up toward the sky."

"I often think how the angels
  Are near us both night and day,
Let us prevent evil passions,
  From driving them far away."

"Just like dear, good little children,
  Let's try to obedient stay,
Of the sins and strifes of this world,
  And we'll hear what angels say."

Heart Thieves.

I John, 3:18.

There is a band of little thieves,
  That often 'round me dart,
And like the wind that takes the leaves,
  They steal away my heart.

Sometimes they catch me unawares,
  And e'er I get my breath,
The heart is gone, I know not where,
  But still I'm not bereft.

Sometimes they come when both my eyes,
  Are fixed upon them straight,
And all at once to my surprise,
  The precious heart they take.

Sometimes they come in regiments,
  By tens, by fives, by twos,
And sometimes even only one,
  But yet the heart is due.

No matter when or how they come,
  Though I know they are thieves.
The heart's door is always open,
  And gladly does receive.

And if they fail to steal my heart,
  The heart is sadly grieved;
And nothing save those little rogues,
  Such sadness can relieve.

Sometimes at home, sometimes at school,
  Sometimes upon the street;
No matter where, it is the rule,
  The heart gives them a greet.

Sometimes it catches one of them,
  And when its not amiss,
The heart turns thief itself—what then?
  It quickly steals a kiss.

And when the heart is so bereft,
  O'er wicked ways of men,
It receives new strength from the thought
  "These little ones don't sin."

And all the influence that I have,
  Which to these thieves is given,
Is pointing out the way that leads
  Their little souls to heaven.

They take the heart at early dawn
  Way off to Paradise,
And show it to the blood-bought throne,
  Around the living Christ.

They take the heart at sultry noon,
  Into a cooling breeze,
Where all of life's hardships make room
  For what we call "heartsease,"

They take the heart at eventide,
  When daily toil is ended;
They take it where the stars abide
  And have its tissues mended.

And when the heart lays down to sleep,
  While in a pensive dream,
These little thieves around it creep,
  And makes the rest serene.

They take the heart at dark midnight,
  And wander far away,
Into the land of pure delight,
  Where midnight is as day.

My friends, I guess you know by now,
  Who these thieves are in part;
The Savior loves the little rogues,
  The children steal my heart.

God Sees.

When I rise at early morn,
Need I fear of any harm—
   God sees.

When I run about and play,
If I 'tempt to go astray—
   God sees.

When my mama whispers low,
" Baby you do so and so"—
   God sees.

If I disobey her rule,
Or if I am rude at school—
   God sees.

If I do the thing that's right,
Whether it be day or night—
   God sees.

If I do a thing that's wrong,
Even though I hide it long—
   God sees.

When I'm through with all the day,
And I kneel at night to pray—
   God sees.

After I am gone to bed,
If I cover up my head—
    God sees.

Even when I'm sound asleep,
While the angels 'round me creep—
    God sees.

So you see I never fear,
God's protection's ever near—
    God sees.

Children and Mother.

I John, 1:4.

Isn't it noble children dear,
To have a mother's voice to hear,
A mother to honor and to love,
And watch that you the right way rove?
Once 'pon a time, I was a child,
And I enjoyed a mother's smile,
Since she's gone to a happy home,
I have felt at times all alone,
But your influence now I feel
Gently across my senses steal,
And undefined, resistless spells,
Bring to me thoughts I cannot tell.

I feel her breath upon my cheek,
And from your letters hear her speak.
Seraphic sounds, more sweetly dear,
Than when from her they met my ear.
Dreams of you, dear children, keep
Your vigils 'round me while I sleep,
And wiping off the sorrowing tears,
Bring back the thoughts of other years.
Bright are the joys your spells create,
They place our minds in happy state,
For music's charm is weak and faint,
To that which children's love can paint.
But now I will not take your time,
For thou art mine, and mine are thine;
Thine by creation's mystic skill,
Which formed and doth sustain us still,
Thine by the more endearing love,
Which sent a Savior from above,
Our souls to save, our lives to bless
With hopes of untold happiness.

Santa Claus on New Years Eve.

It seems to me that all of xmas had gone,
And the new year would be in the coming morn,
And it seems to me 'twas Santa Claus that said:

"I know that the children are safely in bed,
I'll just leave my reindeer and slily steal out,
And take a good peep at the gifts strewn about."
The first place he went to dwelt six reckless boys,
And in a sad plight did he find all their toys,
The drums, it was awful, each one of the six,
Was riddled with holes —there was not a drum
 stick.
A dog with his tail gone, a horse with no head,
A wagon wheel tied to the wagon with thread,
And Santa Claus, you know he felt awful bad,
He stood there and looked disappointed and sad.
And then Santa went where dwelt three tiny
 girls,
All sweet little maidens, with cute dangling
 curls.
He said: "They're not boys with such rough,
 careless ways,
For girls can be happy in much quieter plays,"
But O he was shocked when he entered in
 there,
A doll with both legs off lay under the chair.
A little bird, eyeless, with feathers pulled out,
Reposed on a bed with its tongue in a pout,
The tea sets so scattered that Santa Claus said:
"I feel very sick—I'll go home and to bed."

But some one then asked him to sit in a chair,
And things were explained to him while he was
     there.
They told him that toys wrecked and broken
     but rise
To take on new value in little folk's eyes,
Those drums—'twas a pity—it can't be denied,
The boys longed to see all the noises inside;
The boys found out that they were hollow, no
     doubt,
We all pay big prices some things to find out,
So, Santa. don't plan any vengeance next year,
These toys. worn and broken, are none the less
     dear,
And Santa. all children are not that way,
For some have their toys on the next xmas day.
Then Santa said: "Yes, I'd forgot childish
     days,
I now feel hop'd up, you've explained childish
     plays."
Then Santa Claus was asked to give them a
     speech,
And this is the way that the old man did preach.

*   *   *   *

"We can hear the muffled tread of noiseless
    years,
And they bear the stream of both our smiles
    and tears,
They are loaded down with hopes and dreams
    sublime,
As they come stealing up the scope of time,
We are near the threshold of the open door,
We are treading where we've never trod before
And our days are on a loom and their chimes,
And their warp and woof are past and future
    times.
We are near where the old year is at an end,
And we know that the new will soon begin.
The year that is leaving may be blotted,
But the new one is clear, its page unspotted.
Let us make each day a record page clear,
Then we'll have a clean volume for the year.
Let us grasp now the key of inspiration,
And wind our lives with new determination.
That through the year now coming clear and
    bright,
We'll trust in God and advocate for right."
Then Santa Claus, he nicely bowed his head,
And said the thought of speaking he did dread.

A Chat With the Boys.

I've been a boy myself,
  And with boys I play,
But I'm for solemn chat
  With the boys today.

You are just in prime, boys,
  Life is on ahead,
Its responsibilities
  Never learn to dread.

Never look behind, boys,
  Up and on's the way;
Time enough to look back
  On some future day.

Though the way be long, boys,
  Fight it with a will;
Never stop to look behind
  When climbing up a hill.

First be sure you're right, boys,
  Then with courage strong
Strap your determinations
  And move right along.

You are not always boys,
  Some day you'll be men,
But now is the time, boys,
  For you to begin.

When you're near the top, boys,
  Of the rugged way,
Do not stop to look around,
  But climb, climb away.

Shoot above the crowd, boys,
  Brace yourself and go,
When you meet obstacles
  Strike them with a blow.

Success is at the top, boys,
  Waiting there until
Brain, and pluck, and self respect,
  Have mounted up the hill.

He Knoweth and Loveth You.

Can you count the stars that glimmer
In the azure of the sky?
Do you know how many cloudlets
O'er the world go fleeting by?
God, the Lord, has each one numbered,
Not a star or cloud so small
But His watchful eye has noted,
God, the Father, knows them all.

Do you know how many children
From bright morn to close of day,
Free from sorrow, toil and trouble,
Merry hearted, laugh and play?
God in heaven knows and loves them,
Cares for all they say or do—
Guards them in his tender keeping
And he knows and loveth you.

Industry in Children.

Proverb 22:6.

There's enough, dear children,
  To do in the house,
To keep you as busy
  As a little mouse.

There's enough, dear children,
  To do all about,
And if you will try, you will
  Soon find it out.

There's enough, dear children,
  To do anywhere,
So hurry around and
  Do your full share.

And children, whatever you
   Do, do it well,
People always, in looking it
   Over, can tell.

If mama and papa desire
   You should work,
Go at it cheerfully, don't
   Grow up a shirk.

When you are out with your
   Playmates at play,
Make it as merry as
   Bird songs in May.

And when you grow up to be
   Women and men,
You'll know how to overcome
   Evil and sin.

The future, the future just
   Over the way,
Is patiently looking for
   A better day.

Its hanging, dear children,
   Upon your hand,
And is ready to march
   At your command.

Therefore you are soldiers,
  Captains and guards.
Lead your playmates and be
  Led by your God.

———————————

Vacation's Ending.

I John, 5:21.

Dear children, the hour is near,
  Look 'round in every nook,
And get your slate and pencil,
  And find that absent book.

The summer's sun is sinking
  The nights are getting cool,
Vacation's disappearing,
  It's almost time for school.

A few more days, then Monday,
  You'll hear the ringing bells,
Then you will all be coming
  Vacation news to tell,

You have had lots of play time,
  Lots of recreation;
Take hold of your studies now
  With new determination.

It's very grand, dear children,
   That you can go to school.
Study well each lesson and
   Obey your teacher's rule.

A dear little girl is she,
   Who likes to go to school;
A very naughty boy is he,
   Who daily breaks the rule.

You'll have by day and by night,
   Mama and teacher say:
" Be good my child, do things right,
   And thorough be always."

These words on my ear doth fall,
   And these words I must tell:
" Whatever is done at all,
   Is worth the doing well."

Love your mother and your teacher,
   Love your instruction too,
Love your God who rules above,
   And to yourself be true.

Telephone to Heaven.

A little child with her aunty came
    Into a certain store,
But the merchant was busy waiting
    On those who came before;
The child asked many questions and her
    Aunty would reply:
"That's so and so. You must be quiet,"
    And then she'd give a sigh.

"Well, aunty, wat is dat nittle box wid
    All dem strings tummin down?"
"Why, baby, that's a telephone where they
    Talk all over town."
"I want to talk dat telephone." "No
    Darling, not today."
"Well, net dat man tum talk for me
    I tell him wat to say."

The merchant overheard all this and
    With a pleasant smile,
He thought within himself what he
    Would say to please the child.
And the child had concentrated
    All its thoughts upon the 'phone,
'Till the merchant and the woman
    And the child were all alone.

"Now I can wait on baby," the
  Smiling merchant said,
As he stooped and softly toyed with
  The curly little head.
"I want oo to tall up mama," came
  The answer full and free,
"Wif zo telephone and ast her when
  She's tummin back to me."

"Tell her I so lonesome 'at I don't know
  What to do,
And papa cries so much I dess he must
  Be lonesome too.
Tell her to tum dis eve'ing, tause at night
  I dit so fraid,
Wif no mama here to take me when the
  Night dins to fade.

And ebry day I want her, for my
  Dolly's dot so tored,
From the awful punchen buddy give it
  Wif his little sword,
And aint no body to fix it since
  Mama went away,
And poor little lonesome kittie's ditten
  Thinner every day."

"Sweet child," the merchant murmured as
    He touched its anxious brow.
There's no telephone connection where
    Your mama's living now."
"Aint no telephone in heaven?" and
    Tears came to her eyes,
"I fought dat God had everthing wif
    Him up in the skies."

The woman with a heavy sigh, and
    Child walked out the door,
And the merchant he was puzzled as
    He'd never been before.
And he said, I'll ever strive to make
    Myself a telephone,
Through which the little children can
    All "know as they are known."

Excelsior.

(To the memory of Alma, a little niece, born September
    12th, 1888, died May 30th, 1891.   An angel.)

Rev. 21:11.   19:1.

'Twas in the bleak September,
    The flowers were gone;
When our loving flower,
    Dear Alma was born.

The flowers came and went,
  And came and left once more;
But when they came again,
  Alma thought she'd go.

I asked myself the question,
  "Why take one so dear?"
Spoke my heart full sadly,
  "The answer is not here."

God hath his mysteries,
  Ways that we cannot tell;
He hides them deep like a sleep,
  Of them he loves so well.

She had played, and needed
  A little wayside rest;
Could she have found a better place
  Than her dear Savior's breast?

Her earthly mission was love
  To and from ev'ry one,
She's gone to be rewarded,
  In lands beyond the sun.

Sleep on, precious Alma,
  Take your eternal rest,
Mama and papa're coming
  To take you to their breast.

Weep not beloved parents,
  The Lord, He knoweth best,
Your child's not dead but sleeping
  In God's angelic nest.

She was radiant in beauty,
  Perfect, glorious, bright,
God wanted her for a setting
  In His crown of light.

When the dead now sleep in Jesus,
  Rise in forms that are fair,
Then shall we meet our jewel,
  Our treasure rich and rare.

Our diamond, sapphire, our ruby,
  Our dear little opal of love,
Our pearl, most precious jewel,
  We'll meet her in heaven above.

Where are the Boys.

A question I would like to ask,
To answer it may be a task.
But the thought cannot be masked,
  Where are the boys?

Congregations' service of song,
Thou who workest against all wrong,
Canst thou help us find the throng?
  Where the boys are?

Young People's Club at Baptist church,
Thou who for the boys doeth much,
Canst thou answer for us on such?
  Where are the boys?

Epworth League at Wesley chapel,
Thou who for the boys doth battle,
Canst thou just one answer grapple?
  Where are the boys?

These reply to us in sadness,
We throw out our wings in gladness,
But the boys go by in sadness,
  No boys are here.

Pastors, while at morning service,
Telling men of God's own mercies,
Battling all these earthly curses,
  Where are the boys?

Pastors reply with saddened heart,
The true answer we cannot start,
When the truth we try to impart,
  No boys are there.

Mothers! thou who hast all power,
To begin these human towers,
Canst thou tell at this late hour,
　　Where the boys are?

Mothers with the fashions and styles,
Have not time to lose with the child,
Hence the answer comes with a smile,
　　The boy's all right.

At half past nine o'clock at night,
Up and down the streets in a flight,
Some at play and others in fights,
　　There are the boys.

On the corners they congregate,
In wicked oaths they conversate,
With a cigarette puff they state,
　　We are not boys.

Thus they are moving down life's stream,
Grasping all things low and mean,
Soon we will hear a mother scream
　　Where is my boy?

This is the way they get their start,
The county farms will get their part,
Then we hear mother's broken heart.
　　Where is my boy?

Then they wish time in its flight
Could make him a child for one night,
O! on what a different plight,
    They'd start their boy.

Too late, too late, will come the cry,
Neglected days have hastened by.
Hence we will hear both sobs and
    sighs—
    Where is my boy?

In the year of nineteen ten,
There'll be a mighty call for men,
What can we give as answer then?
    Where were the boys?

The nation's cancer makes a dust,
And moral virtue calls out thus,
Mothers, thou who hast all the trust,
    Where are the boys?

Mothers! You have power to save,
Down life's long stream you start the
    wave,
Mothers! keep not our minds enslaved.
    Where are the boys?

Children's Day.

I John, 4: 4.

Children, when you read that sweet story of old,
　　When Jesus was here among men,
How he called little children as lambs to his fold,
　　Wouldn't you liked to have been with him
　　　　then?

Though you could not see His kind look when
　　he spoke,
　　You can only read the story
You are greater today while under his yoke,
　　Than all of Solomon's glory.

Though before our time death frost came to lie
　　Upon his warm and mighty heart,
And it quenched His bold and tender eye,
　　His spirit did not all depart.

That spirit now from thousands of pens,
　　Is thrown upon the lucid page,
It's moving, it shakes the heart of men,
　　In this golden, yet sinful age.

It's showing the children how to go,
　　To witness a part of His love,
And if we will seek Him here below,
　　We will see Him and hear Him above.

He's gone away, only to prepare,
   For those whose sins are forgiven,
And many children have gathered there,
   For such is the kingdom of Heaven.

Come, look in my eyes little children,
   And tell me through all the long day,
Have you thought of your God and your Savior,
   Who keepeth from sin all your ways?

When you go to rest little children,
   Right over your innocent sleep,
Unseen by your vision, His angels
   Their watch through the darkness doth keep.

They heareth e'en the cry of the sparrows,
   They careth for great and for small;
In life and in death, little children,
   Their love is the truest of all.

Then we'll pray that the love which guideth,
   The lambs that they loveth so well,
May lead you that in life's bright morning,
   Beside the still waters you'll dwell.

Since there's a world that's beyond the grave,
   And children are all hastening there;
While you are in your youthful strength,
   Incline your dear hearts to prayer.

Put your trust not in this world, children,
  Which has for you thousands of charms,
Though they catch the fancy a moment,
  To the soul they all doeth harm.

We are faced by sinful influences,
  But our Savior was crucified;
For your sins and my sins dear children,
  He suffered, He languished, He died.

But He went and buried His sorrows,
  Knowing that we all had our share;
And He opened a crystal fountain,
  And bid children enter there.

You children were made for life's battle,
  And God's sword is girt on your thigh;
And the purpose of God is overthrown,
  If you only linger and sigh.

For our lives are coinages of heaven,
  To be spent in a coinage of love;
'Till all the realms of earth below,
  Are as pure as the realms above.

We are strangers, we are pilgrims,
  But Christ our eternal brother,
Whispers from out His blood-bought throne,
  "Little children, love one another."

I wish that your thoughts so heavenly were,
  And your hearts to Christ so given;
That all our toils, our love, our care,
  Might lead us nearer to heaven.

Were it in my power dear children,
  To set all of sin's pinions free;
Your paths should be paved more smoothly,
  Throughout time to eternity.

Let us all try daily to forge a key,
  To open the gates of heaven,
If we make that key the hearts of men,
  The bolt will be backward driven.

The Simple Reason.

III John, 1:4.

The sweet month of May was drawing to a
      close,
The month of hope and promise, of leaves
And sunshine that clothes the earth
With smiles, but fills many hearts with tears,
By calling the victims of consumption to its
Green gloom. It was the evening of the
Holy Sabbath. The public worship was near
Over, and never since has my heart been
So deeply touched as by the songs they sang.

The children's voices sounded above all others.
   They were singing, sweetly singing,
   It was a lovely Sabbath day,
   And the evening air was ringing,
   About the little child, Angel May.
   They sang of her stately sadness,
   How 'twas whispered in heaven afar,
   How she asked the watchman one favor.
   To set the beautiful gates ajar,
   "Only a little, I pray thee,
   Set the beautiful gates ajar."
   "I can hear my mother weeping,"
   Said the child in a trembling tone,
   Feeling that heaven she couldn't enjoy,
   With mother on earth alone.
   She felt that when the gate was closed,
   Her mother couldn't see her so far;
   So she cried, "O angel give me the key,
   And I'll set the gate ajar,
   Only a little I pray thee,
   Set the beautiful gate ajar."

   The warden knew not a mother's worth,
   Hence could not feel for the child,
   And prompted by heavenly duty,
   He answered her with a smile.

And when the child impressed it,
Speaking of mother afar,
The warden answered "I dare not
Set the beautiful gates ajar,"
In a low calm way I dare not,
"Set the beautiful gate ajar."
Then up rose Mary the blessed,
The mother of the Savior of men,
Who knew the child's young feelings,
Who had motherly feelings within,
She laid her hand on the angel,
Whose feelings were just at par.
The warden, seeing her expression,
Set the beautiful gate ajar—
Just for the sake of the mother,
Set the beautiful gate ajar.

Turned was the key in the portal,
Fell ringing the golden bar,
And, lo, in the little child's fingers,
Stood the beautiful gate ajar.

With exultation I was about to rise when
A stir was made, and a man rose whom
I can never forget. He was an old man
Upon whose frame the years of a
Century had left their traces; while

As snow his white beard hung upon his
Breast; and although the lower part of his
Face was sunken by extreme age, his eyes
Beamed with a fadeless benevolence and his
Brow had scarcely a wrinkle.   They told me
Afterward, that he was the most loved
Companion of Christ and in sweetness of tem-
Per most like the children.

    Unable to support himself, he was carried
Forward in the arms of his friends to the
Little rostrum at the end of the room.
All rose to greet him, and even little children
Looking up into his face with affectionate
Joy, as he whispered "Bless the children."
Having reached the stand, he attempted to
Speak, but failing, sunk into the arms
Of friends.

      Eyes swam in tears,
      Hearts melted in sorrow,

After a little, he revived.   They raised
Him up again.   He looked around like a
Father taking his last farewell, then
Stretched forth his hands above the group,
And, while tears ran down his cheeks,
He cried with tremulous voice,

      "Little children love one another."

He could say no more. It was his last
Sermon.   He looked around upon them again
With a smile of divine sweetness and
His lips moved, but we heard nothing.   His
Eyes fell upon me and with a feeble gesture
He beckoned me to him and seemed to read
My countenance.   "Sir," said I, "You and
The children almost persuadest me to
Be a Christian.   You are fixing to
Leave me.   The children will be with me,
We are to battle life for each other.   I
Pray thee leave me thy grace."
Grasping my hand he said, "I leave
You seven words, give them to the
Children, they are Faith, Hope, Charity,
Peace, Joy, Truth and Love."
"Father," said I, "can't you tell me what is
    faith?"
He whispered distinctly—

 "Faith is that which you see descending
 Down from the realms of celestial light,
 Something that's on the cross depending
 Guiding children through this life aright."
And what is hope?

 "Hope has a sight which nerves the weary,
 And all of its brightness in luster shines,

It lights the path when all life seems dreary,
It cheers when all our strength declines."
And what is charity?
"Charity comes in and helps soothe the dying,
Its ears are open to the orphan's wail,
It hears the voice of the homeless crying,
It feeds the hungry and protects the frail."
And what is peace?
"Peace is a calm, meek, tender glory,
That fills our souls with the pride of life,
It helps the youth and the age when hoary,
It is free from passion, from war, and strife."
And what is joy?
Joy comes pure as a fragrant flower,
Its blossoms are scattered along life's stream,
It cheers the heart in its youthful hours,
And lulls men's cares like a merry dream."
And what is truth?
"Truth comes in a majestic splendor,
And its light shines in all honest souls,
It makes men just, in their nature tender,
It gives all strength to character it holds."
I will not ask you what is love, for I believe
That is a combination of these six.
The mortal spasm now grasped him. Once
More he spake, but it was with the energy

Of strong health, "Even so, Lord Jesus take
Me"—he was asleep in death. I
Turned to leave and

A poor wayfaring man of grief
Was standing by my side,
Who sued my conscience for relief,
His wounded side I eyed.

He uttered not a single word,
But showed his nail'd print hand;
He saw my heart was so bestir'd,
He said "You understand."

He said "go to some mountain,
And call the children near;
You dip them in a fountain,
And teach their heart to fear."

He then left me. I am now a
Christian. Children I have many things to
Tell you, and through grace I intend
To tell them yet.
A week passed and one of the blandest
Mornings in June that ever the sun rose
Upon, I visited his library and found
On a tablet these words: "Jesus is very
Precious to my soul, my all in all, and I
Expect to be saved by free grace through
His atoning blood. This is my testimony."

I left the room resolving within
Myself to make his testimony my
Testimony and to

Love the children just as he did,
Who for love once sweetly pleaded;
Trust and guide, and never doubt
Build a wall of love about.

But I've always loved the jewels,
Always thought that it was cruel,
To efface their youthful beauty
It has been a life-time duty.

Yes, I love them, I remember,
May is not like cold December.
If I've words of rage and madness,
Always check it from their gladness.

When my heart is filled with kindness,
And to evil shows its blindness;
Then it's time to turn my whole heart
Into the porte called children's mart.

When I'm thinking of my Savior,
When I'm seeking good behavior;
When I look for earthly angels,
Then I with the children mingle.

When the general roll is thunder'd,
If among the saints I'm number'd,
I will search that place of honor,
'Till I find the children's corner.

"And now little children, abide in him; that, when he shall appear, we may have confidence, and not be ashamed before him at his coming."—I John, 2:28.

PART III.

Ajax' Ordeals on Lynching.

Ajax' Dream.

Ajax of the Southland
　　Was walking out one day,
Enraptured did his spirit seem,
Inspired by some poetic theme,
　　Or heavenly array.

His gaze was running forward,
　　When sudden toward the sky,
A buzzard rose upon his wings,
From off a dark and ghastly thing
　　Which startled Ajax' eyes.

A hideous corpse he noticed,
　　He shudders, standing there—
His spirit feels a sharp recoil,
From that which taints the air and soil
　　From lack of burial care.

The lynchers had been there
　　And killed a Negro man;
They would not let his kindred come,
Nor even friends his corpse entomb,
　　But left it on the sand.

He almost turns to leave it—
    But stops and turns again,
That carcass there was once the home
Of some sad soul now doomed to roam
    Perhaps in endless pain.

And so this trembling Ajax
    The duty does not shirk,
But with his unaccustomed hands
Piles on the corpse the dirt and sand,
    And it was tedious work.

When Ajax' work was o'er
    He said with tearful eyes,
"This country, call'd the 'land of free,'
Has no protection here for me,
    But whither shall we fly?"

He thought of Afric's jungles,
    Where his ancestors roamed,
He thought of all the foreign lands,
Where he thought man could be a man
    And have protected homes.

A ship was there in waiting,
    Her prows turned toward the sea.
So Ajax said, at break of day,
I'll take this ship and sail away
    In search of liberty.

He wended his way homeward
　　His mind was all afright,
He made a hasty trip to bed,
And tried to doze away the dead,
　　He passed a restless night.

But while he slept a spirit,
　　Before him seemed to stand—
The soul whose body on the beach
He covered from the buzzard's reach,
　　Who spoke with warning hand.

"Ajax." said the spirit,
　　"Listen to a friend's command!
Thou hast in mind to sail the sea
In search of free-born liberty,
　　This is thy native land!"

So when Ajax awoke—
　　He formed a resolution,
He said this is my native land,
And if I make myself a man,
　　There'll be a revolution.

And then he closed by saying:
　　"I think I know the sequel,
I'll patronize my fellow man,
And lend him all the aid I can,
　　And thus build up my people."

Ajax' Second Dream.

I dreamed I was with the lynchers,
And in their arms I lay.
Ah me! has the vision vanished,
Have the demons passed away?
They are like a pack of hell-hounds,
They seek an innocent man,
And simply on his color
He dies at their command.

Sing to me songs of slavery,
They will cool me after my sleep,
And with freedom's odors fan me,
Till into my veins they creep,
For my heart is hot and restless,
And all of the lynchers' crimes—
The hundreds of hanging bodies
Are dancing before my mind.

My soul! this lifeless nature,
Oppresses my brain and heart;
Oh! for a storm and thunder,
To sunder this world apart!
Stop singing, please—I hate it,
But take up a buckle and sword,
And clash these human demons,
Till this lynching world is stirred.

Now leave me, and take from my chamber,
This wretched mosquito, and tell
The people how much he annoys me,
With his silly, tinkling bells.
Its strange, but my nerves he vexes,
A thing without blood or brain,
But ask it first please to help me
To tear the lynchers in twain.

I long for the jungles of Africa,
Among the wild beasts to roam,
Where the hissing of the reptiles,
Will make me feel at home:
In a vision I was transported,
To Africa in a day,
And through the jungles of memory,
Loosen'd my fancy to play.

I wandered through the jungles,
I played with the crocodiles,
And toyed the head of the hissing asp,
As we often do a child:
The elephant trumpeting started,
When he heard my footsteps near,
The kangaroo fled wildly,
Crying in distressing fear.

And I heard a wild mate roaring,
As the shadows of night came on,
To snooze in the brush beside me,
And the thoughts of my sleep were gone.
Then I roused myself from slumber
And sprang to my trembling feet,
Anxious for some one to soothe me,
I wandered my mate to greet.

We grasped each other on meeting,
And rolled upon the sand,
And tried our best to kill each other—
How powerful he was and grand.
Then with all his might he seized me,
With a wild, triumphant cry,
That sounded like the lynchers' yell,
And the Negro's wail and sigh.

We grappled and worried together,
For we both had rage that was rude,
And his teeth as they sank into my flesh,
Drew forth the lynch-escaped blood.
But I had courage to fight him,
For we were but foe to foe,
While the lynchers come by hundreds,
To defend we have no show.

Other wild beasts were vicious,
The lion and the grizzly bear
Fought for me in the moonlight,
While I lay crouching there.
Then down to the river we loitered,
Where the young fawns came to drink,
And my beast friends sprang upon them,
Ere they had time to shrink.

The wild beast in the jungles,
Had tenderer, softer hearts,
Than America's Anglo-Saxon,
In civilized Christian marts;
Would that I had the power
To touch the hearts of men,
And with the aid of wild beast
Reveal this wretched sin.

Ajax' Fright.

There's a dreadful horror 'bout me,
   That nothing drives away;
It's with me in my night dreams,
   It's with me every day.

It makes the night appear so short,
  The bed is hard and cold;
It makes the days appear so long
  To both the young and old.

Must I arise from out my bed,
  And start my daily work?
The lynchers, just for meanness, will
  My head from body jerk.

To die like a man by gun or shield,
  Such a death I do not fear;
No other death 'ld be worst to feel,
  Than to leave my loved ones here.

But fear of being lynched for naught
  Makes all one's senses start;
To be chased by hounds and hell-hounds
  Draws pangs to bleeding hearts.

I hear the hell-hounds yelping,
  They're coming 'cross the plain;
With bloodshot eyes and gnashing teeth,
  For blood of a Negro's veins.

I've never harmed a white man,
  They can't be after me;
But oh! when they're blood thirsty,
  Innocence is no plea.

There's stirring in my back yard,
  There's fumbling under my floor,
Great God they seem to smell me!
  The lynchers are at my door!

Ajax' Soliloquy.

Riches, which once I held in light esteem,
And inspired me—now I laugh to scorn;
And lust of fame which was an ideal dream,
Has vanished from me with the morn.

When in my solitary room I sit,
And try to see where life presents a bloom;
Not one fair dream before my mind's eye flits,
But hateful thoughts enwrap my soul in gloom.

My heart aches, instead of night rest, my
        dreams
Are anxious, that a cup filled up with drugs
For me to drink, and leave the world unseen.
And go and be a feast to hungry bugs.

Would I could fade, dissolve, go and forget
That I upon the earth was ever known,
For all these crimes, the fever and the fret,
All we can do is hear each other groan.

There is something painful and sad to see,
'Twould shock the red man looking for a scalp:
A human body hanging from a tree,
A white man's victim that had been entrap'd.

I often pray, but the only touching prayer,
That from my heart doth move my lips for me,
Is, "You may have the heart that now I bear.
But give my mind and body liberty."

O spirit, O spirit of the other land,
Turn here your voice and in a whisper say:
"O Ajax! O Ajax! come from that stand,
And dwell with me in a brighter day."

I'm pond'ring, I'm wond'ring, I'm thinking,
If this world intends to ever get right;
It's reeling, it's shaking, it's sinking,
Let my soul join the blue bird's flight.

Ajax' Kindred's Soliloquy.

In Africa.

The thoughts of the future doth puzzle my mind,
And O how I shudder at flitting of time;
It seems that it's hast'ning that dreadful day,
When no where in this dull earth I can stay.
The powers of Europe are taking my land,
And sifting it out at their own command.

They do not attempt to civilize me,
But use all their efforts to make me flee.
Where in this broad domain can I fly,
My body to rest and my mind satisfy?
That land called the Star Spangled Banner of
        free,
Toward which all the nations at one time did
        flee,
My countryman Ajax who dwells over there,
Relates that which straightens my sun kinked
        hair,
He tells me they lynch, tar and burn the Negro,
And mangle them worse than the cruel Nero,
He tells me to stay here and dodge the wild
        beast,
It's easier than being the lynchers' love feast,
The isles of the sea are all filled up they say,
I wish a new mountain would rise in a day;
The fox and the panther, the birds of the air,
They all have a home in this world somewhere,
The sun shines resplendent in its bright degree,
Dame nature is pleasant, all happy but me,
I long for the wings of the blue bird of flight,
To flee from this plain and in mid ocean light,
And there put an end to these heart-bleeding
        sighs,

And banish the tears from my long weeping
    eyes.
O God! is the time ever coming again
When I can see peace in this broad domain?
If not take me now in the palm of thy hand,
And fling me away from this blood-shedding
    land.
And if I don't land in thy mansions all fair,
Just fling me until I am nothing but air.
The lynchers, the lynchers are here by the
    throng!
My Savior, my Savior, O, why was I born.

Ajax' Monument.

When in the shadow of the tomb,
    My heart shall rest,
Please lay me where spring flowers bloom
    On earth's green breast.

Please never in vaulted box place
    My lifeless frame,
For it is not the best of grace,
    Yes, I am sane.

In some sweet village of the dead
   I'd like to sleep,
Where flowers may deck my little bed,
   Where angels creep.

And if the children in their roam
   Know not the spot:
Enough if but by love alone,
   I'm not forgot.

But I'm a Negro and I need
   Not so lament,
For never did a lyncher's creed
   Say "monument."

My God, will the time ever be,
   When I can have
Pure thoughts without the lynchers' glee
   To make me swear?

Ajax' Song.

(Tune: "Tenting on the Old Camp Ground.")

We are thinking today of the loved ones lost,
   Gone through the lynchers' hand:
Of the innocent men who have gone across
   The bridge where villains stand.

CHORUS.

Many are the hearts that are mourning today,
    Mourning for the loved ones mobbed,
Many are the eyes full of tears that say,
    Why are we left in sobs?
Help us to say, "Humbly we pray,
    Father, is it brighter ahead?"

We are hoping today that the Christian world,
    Will yet see the matter straight;
And will see that this question is all unfurl'd,
    Before time replies, "too late!"

     CHORUS: Many are the hearts, etc.

We are praying today to our God on high,
    To wrestle this lynching age;
To listen to the widow's and orphan's cry,
    That's caused by this outrage.

     CHORUS: Many are the hearts, etc.

We are weeping today but the hour will come,
    When the lynchers all shall see
That America is the Negro's home,
    And here he's bound to be.

     CHORUS: Many are the hearts, etc.

Ajax' Meditations.

If I should die
Today or tomorrow,
And my soul fly,
Into bliss or sorrow,
Would any who never saw my face,
Know that on this earth I had filled a place?

If I should sail
Away on some great ship,
And in a gale
Should end my earthly trip,
Would anyone while riding o'er the waves,
Remember me while in my wat'ry grave?

If I should stray,
Way off in the wild woods,
And be the prey
To vicious wild beasthood,
Would future men while lev'ling down the plain,
Know that I'd ever been in this domain?

If I, at home,
Were quietly sleep in bed;
And lynchers roamed,
To tar and burn my head,
They would prevent my friends from burying me
Could future men say that I used to be?

If when I'm dead,
The future children come,
With joyous tread
And human beating drums,
Will they while either at their work or play,
Remember that poor Ajax had a day?

Songsters will sing,
While I am dead and gone;
Their echo'll ring,
And thrill the living throng,
Will any songs remind the living men,
That poor Ajax upon the earth has been?

A cent'ry hence,
While boys and girls in school,
Upon the bench
Obey the teacher's rule,
Will any book show them the deeds and acts,
Of trembling, poor, despis'd, oppress'd Ajax?

God hold my hand,
And give me power to write,
Give me command,
That I may say what's right.
I'll write a book before I leave this land,
To show the world that Ajax was a man.

A Mother's Rage.

Fruits of Lynching.

A mother stood at the river brink
  Holding in her arms a dear child,
'Twas all on earth that the mother had,
  And she said with a sacred smile:
"Your father did all a man could do
  To live for you and for me;
But the wicked lynchers murdered him,
  Irrespective of mother's plea."

She says, "I know whereof I speak,
  In the sight of these my own eyes,
Your father said in a mournful tone:
  'Dear wife, kiss the baby good-bye,'
And that was the last I heard of him;
  I knew not the lynchers' plan.
The world is witness to one true fact,
  Thy father was an honest man.

But honesty in this fast age,
  In regards to the dusky race
Has carried many 'cross the dark stage,
  And brought to the whites a disgrace.
If this mode of death is continued,
  Why should I leave you, my dear boy,
To have your life blotched with such sights,
  Such a life you cannot enjoy!

My child, I am almost tempted now
  To throw thee into this river,
And let thy soul go wandering back
  To Him who is the great forgiver.
For then thy mother will be satisfied
  That thou art in God's tender care,
For another death like thy father's
  Thy mother, she can never bear.

And then, my child when you have passed
  Beyond earth's shadows and its teachings,
When Paradise is reached at last,
  Brought to you by the Lord's entreating,
When starry crowns shall deck your brow,
  And white robes to you be given,
My child, you can't imagine now,
  How sweet 'twill be in heaven.

The "many mansions" high in air
  Will gleam with more than earthly splendor,
And the shining angels, pure and fair,
  Will greet you with a love most tender;
Your head in grief shall never bow
  But rapturous joy'll to you be given,
My child, you can't imagine now
  How sweet 'twill be in heaven.

But oh? my child my heart repines, -
  How horrible would be the guilt
When in after years it comes to mind
  That your blood was by mother spilt;
My child, I cannot bear to think
  Of throwing thee into the tide;   .
But oh, the lynchers! the lynchers!
  The mother fainted and died.

Ajax' Bashfulness.

I was once out of social circles,
As bashful as a young man could be;
And I wondered if all society
Could make a socialist of me.

I wandered on in my bashfulness,
Nothing socially good could I see;
And the thought filled my heart with sad-
      ness,
No social redemption for me.

I went to a town on probation,
And my bashfulness followed me,
And while in deep meditation,
A voice gently whispered to me.

It was the voice of a social club,
That was speaking so kindly to me;
And I heard its social improvements
Saying tenderly, "come unto me."

I went to the club very shyly,
They gladly accepted of me,
But I told them I was so bashful,
A socialist I never could be.

And I found that while it was social,
Some other things they'd review;
There was moral's tie and culture's trend.
They ever had in view.

The first time that they called on me,
I didn't have very much blood,
But all I had to my head did flee,
And I felt like social mud.

And when I got through they all clap'd me,
'Twas not about what I said;
But they were, through sympathy,
Clapping the blood from my head.

We next had the social jubilee,
And from my heart I wondered;
If any girl there would talk to me—
A simple, social blunder.

And when I came to myself again,
I was drifting down the tide;
I was in the boat for the social port,
With a lady on each side.

Ajax Looks Beyond.

I have tried to be contented
In this land of vale and tears,
When I think how Christ, the Savior,
Suffered here without a fear;
But the way that I am treated
In this low slough of despond,
Makes me long to be transported
To the calm, unknown beyond.

I am longing for a moment
When I can this country leave;
For some unknown, peaceful city,
Where they never sigh or grieve,
Where the mansions glow with beauty,
Which to mortals is unknown;
I am waiting, I am longing
In those brighter realms to roam.

I am longing for the breaking
Of the day when I'll be free,
And can leave behind the heartaches,
And toward my Savior flee;
When I shall to lynching horrors,
In this cold world bid adieu,
I am waiting, I am longing,
And my race is waiting too.

Ajax Votes for McKinley.

Ajax went out to vote
    On election day;
White man was standing 'round,
    Things had gone his way.

Ajax had heard before
    How the white man done,
Made Negroes vote with him
    Or,—he had a gun.

White man said to Ajax,
    "Well, how do you stand?"
Ajax said to white man,
    "Straight republican."

White man said to Ajax,
   "Leave the poles at once."
Ajax said to white man,
   "You must be a dunce."

White man said to Ajax,
   "You don't mean to go?"
Ajax said to white man,
   "While I'm living—No!"

Ajax said, quite raging,
   "This thing's got to stop,
Bossing Negroes' voting,
   No more'll be a sop."

White man saw that Ajax
   Was not like the rest;
Could not be bluffed away
   With a little jest.

White man said to Ajax,
   "Why are you so bold?"
Ajax said to white man,
   "My rights to control."

White man said to Ajax,
   "I don't mean to fight."
Ajax said to white man,
   "I'm for peace and right."

White man said to Ajax,
  "Drop your war-like game."
Ajax said to white man,
  "When you do the same."

White man said to Ajax
  "What'll you do to me?"
Ajax said to white man,
  "Hit me and you'll see!"

White man said to Ajax,
  "This will never do."
Ajax said to white man,
  "Sir, the same to you."

White man said to Ajax,
  "I'll the diet try."
Ajax said to white man,
  "Thank you, so will I."

Ajax showed the white man
  He knew how to fight;
White man showed to Ajax
  He could treat him right.

Ajax' Conclusion.

My friends, our race is ostracised,
Long standing tears are in our eyes,
And we as meek and humble doves,
Endure it all with smiles and love.
And those who try to crush us down
Return our smiles in hateful frowns,
So we must rise and strike a blow,
When e'er these demons block our door.

As long as we retreat from them,
They'll use us as their limber-jim,
But if we punishments resist,
The white man'll know that we exist,
And if we all united stand,
We can our rights as men demand;
But we must show determination,
Instead of meek disconsolation.

The red man showed that he would fight,
This country gave him certain rights,
They never lynch an Indian chief,
They know his friends come to relief,
The foreigner from 'cross the sea,
Has all the rights of liberty,
Because if humans take his scalp,
His countrymen will raise a scrap.

The rattlesnake, the white man dreads,
And on his body will not tread,
Because he knows the rattlesnake,
If touched, will to'ard the toucher make.
The harmless ant upon the ground,
Men trample on without a frown,
If we resist, we'll gain respect,
If we unite 'twill take effect.

There must be some blood shed by us,
When Southern brutes begin to fuss,
Some Brown and Turner've got to die,
To picture to the demon's eye
The fact that we are in this land
To stay, 'till God gives us command
To move away, and until then,
We must be recognized as men.

We made the South-land with our toil,
And we intend to share the spoil,
But sometimes it seems just as well
To have a residence in hell.
Poor men are cut and burnt like fuel,
The country does not call it cruel.
Someone must rouse this base-ball age,
To overcome this black outrage.

Who's more fit to defend this right,
Than we who've seen these wicked sights?
Stern freedom's voice bids us arise,
Our patient ways she does despise,
Contentment makes real life decay,
Brave discontent brings brighter day,
What we are now, the past has made,
The future's on our shoulders staid.

Ajax is Chastised.

Ajax, in the stillness of the night,
   Lie down and take thy rest;
Live in the dreams of the starry light
   As the bird in its nest.

This world is filled with sorrow and shame,
   With sin, with tumult rife;
But as metal is fused by the flame,
   So men are made by strife.

Ere long from now, thy feet may turn
   From this distressing mood;
So lose the thought that men are burned,
   And help to make life good.

And Ajax, though it wounds and grieves,
  We grow strong by lees of pain,
So shelter your heart against the thieves,
  And be thyself again.

You have your life, why not be glad?
  For the gift of life is good;
But the lessons of life are great and sad
  To thy dear brotherhood.

So turn your back on the sinful ways,
  And blend the race together;
Let us unite for a brighter day,
  And help to make life better.

Ajax at the Centennial.

1897.

Ajax went over to Nashville,
To attend the great centennial;
And a white man asked him rashly
About the race in general.

"Ajax, tell me the whole sequel:
Your father was my father's slave,
And now you stand as my equal,
On this educational wave."

And Ajax paused for a moment,
Slightly hanging down his head;
And then from the depth of conscience,
These are the words that he said:

"You know it was sixteen-nineteen,
When my first African brother,
Sailed over here in a canteen,
And called America his mother.

He climbed up degradation's hill,
Two hundred and fifty years;
And over the Israelitic rills,
He waded through heartaches and tears.

In his efforts to leave degradation,
He was cramped, doomed in a cell;
Dishearten'd, discontent'd, discourag'd,
By a prejudice born in hell.

But through God's work, who guides
    man's life,
The world's second Moses came;
And through the sea of civil strife,
Brought freedom instead of shame.

From there we started out in life,
To make a mark as a race;
But someone's ever causing strife,
Bringing on us a disgrace.

You take the thousand oppressions,
That are hurled into our face;
And change them to progression,
Then we will be a race.

My sir, it is a well-known fact,
That the Negroes' aim is high,
And if they'll stop holding him back,
He'll reach them unless he dies.

He's in the national government,
He's been a military man;
And in these United States,
He's been surveyor of lands.

He's widely known in medicine,
He's faced millions as teacher;
Thundered his eloquence at the bar,
He can't be excelled as preacher.

And in hundreds of newspapers,
He tones up ideas and thoughts;
In connection with his people,
To show what they have wrought.

As for a Southern laboring man,
His equal cannot be found;
And to find a regular Negro tramp,
You must search the country 'round.

In scholarship he's stood the test,
In the institute's at home;
And 'cross the sea—without a jest.
His eloquence is known.

He's writing poetry books and prose,
To scatter over the land;
To show the depth from which he 'rose,
The height where now he stands.

A hundred thousand students now,
Behind the study desk;
Have fix'd a frown upon their brow,
They will not be oppressed.

I think I see the coming time,
When this curs'd lynching land;
Will see the Negro's worth sublime,
And claim him as a man.

And my dear sir, fifty years hence,
When your grandchildren stand;
Ajax grandchildren's recompense,
Will show an equal man.

A hundred years from now my friend,
Could you and I peep back;
We cannot tell your children then,
From those of poor Ajax.

Ajax' Appeal to America.

My country, noble spectre of the past;
Along thy rivers, and within thy vales,
There breathes a deep-toned voice, that tells
    of days,
When thou wert called the country of the free—
Admired and frequented; when pilgrim'd hosts
Trod thy sanctomed shores, and music filled
The air with freedom. Broad hearts of men
Were thine, in bonds of union; and around,
The voice of love and happiness arose.
Voluptuous life enkindled every heart—
But as time moved on in silence,
A dreadful change took place,
The great Abe. Lincoln wept, he saw the wreck
That slavery scattered 'round him—and he
    mourned
To think that scenes so bright should fade so
    soon.
Thou wast a marvelous country, ere the star
That lit the way to Bethlehem, gleamed the
    east.
And heralded a Savior—and perhaps,
Thy shores resounded with the hum of men,
When Ajax on the Afric shores did live.

Thou wast a brilliant mystery--and from far,
The nations of the earth poured into thee.
Thou prospered well, now four wars,
Stamped upon thy flag, but these four wars,
And four times four large wars of ancient times,
Could not shed blood enough to cover up
The principle that underlies the greatest
Of all wars, that's waged by thee 'gainst thine,
And thou could'st with one stroke exterminate.

Thou claimes't to be a Christian country,
And rankest with highly civilized countries,
And there is nothing in the category of crime,
Or in the history of savages to surpass those--
Fiendish, blood-chilling horrors perpetrated
        against
My people by your Christians. The southern
        mob,
When in its rage feeds its vengance by shoot-
        ing,
Stabbing and burning men alive, which only
Some disgusting birds and beasts, would do.
And to plead "not guilty" is a waste of time,
For when the mob's will has been accomplish-
        ed,
And its thirst for blood has by its bands been
        quenched.

And the victim is speechless, silent, dead,
Then the mobocratic amusers have the ear of
The world all to themselves, and the world
Listens to them—because thy noble govern-
        ment,
Planted by the Pilgrim Fathers, Defended by
Noble Washington and regenerated by God-
        sent Lincoln—
Urges it on and it widens as the waters
Of the Missisippi entering the great gulf.
And those amusers who so bravely kill, would
        flee
Like Phantoms if brought face to face with that
Great law on which thy forces move.
                        The foreigner
Who looks across the sea, and never comes,
Thinks thou art great, magnanimous and brave,
And we have heartily hoped that this estimate,
Would soon cease to be contradicted. Instead
        our
Confidence in thy nobility as a nation has been
Shaken—and the future all looks dark
And troubled. This tends to dim the lustre
Of thy noble name and to obliterate the
Cause of liberty which thou hast sung to the
        world.

Thy moral sense is now on a decline and we
May well ask the question " how low " some of
Thy safe guards are swept away. Supreme
Courts are surrendered, State sovereignity is
Restored, Civil rights are destroyed, men
        are
Lynched like beast of the forest. What next?
Emmigration wont save us for we are convinced
That this is our native land. Neither will
Colonization redeem us for we are colonized
To day upon the land that gave us birth.
Think, O America, of the sublime and glorious
Truths with which, at thy birth, thou saluted
A listening world. Thy voice was then the
Trump of an archangel, summoning oppres-
        sion,
And time-honored tyranny to inherit the sweet
Freedom of thy shores. The oppressed flock-
        ed to thee.
Crowned heads trembled, toiling millions
Clapped for joy. Brotherhood, equality. liber-
        ty,
And truth were the inviting features.
You redeemed the world from the bondage
Of ages, was it to enslave them again?
And not only to enslave them but slaughter

Worse than the unspeakable Turks do
The Armenians, or the dread Spaniards
Do the Cubans. Are the horrors of Siberia,
Against the thriving Jew to be exceeded
By thy Christian crimes?

                                    To thee
One came in humble guise, upon whose brow
A sweet harmonious peace in beauty shone.
Towards portals of peace, the heroic Ida Wells
Reposed within thy house, and talked of right.
Oh, had thy powers then but heard her voice,
And trod the way she pointed,—then with thee
This darkness would have ended,—and this
        crime
Which hangs about thy neck, would hang no
        more.
But, lacking the warm hope that filled her
        breast,
To cheer the rose-lipped nymph in her great
        work,
She down-cast minded, but determined soul
Kept a superior thought and crossed the sea.
From thy great name she could have told
Of the bright mansions in the freeman's land:
O'er which no night descended. From her lips,
The foreign nations could have learned of love

And friendship, such as this lynched land of ours
Can show no sign or symbol.

                                    Ida's faith
Was weak and wavering, and she opened up
The eyes of Christian nations far across the
Sea who've been in darkness and misled
For quite a while. And they do think that
When a nation's moral tone is on the decline,
We well may wonder what will be the depth.
Thou art declining noble state! and the breath
Of pestilence among thy lynching towns
Sweeps to and fro, and in the place,
Where Lincoln's armies rode,   there   lies   a
          shade,
That of late days have gathered like a pall.
A midnight hangs upon thee—not alone
This lynching crime, but the dim eclipse
Of moral desolation. Heaven's frown
Is visible around thee.   Rise! thou wreck
Of self downfall, and call upon thy God—
If alone, so that those within thy bound,
This land so dark and cheerless. may not
See the bright day of hope in gloom go down!
But where protection, which is life and light,
Broods ever like the grandure of the stars,
That studs the summer skies of boundless
          blue.

Ajax' Death.

(A DRAMA.)

DRAMATIS PERSONÆ:

ELI.

RAMECH, wife of ELI.

AJAX, their son.

JOBEL their infant child.

Time—between 1890 and 1900, A. D.

Scene—A mountain near the Mississippi river
  where no one inhabits.

ELI.

Its awful the way our people are lynched.
Its a shame we are driven to this
Desolate place to save our lives, simply
Because I had some influence among
My people and refused to use it to
Suit the white man and injure my people.
I have invoked my god without response.
What else can I do?

RAMECH.

Name not thy gods, for I condemn them.
For they have urged to curse thy destiny,
And brought on us this desolate spot as home.

ELI.

Don't condemn me, O Ramech! I may err
In my imploring, but should I not pray?

RAMECH.

Pray to the God above. You know I oft
Remind you of our wickedness, and warn
You of this Southern god, the white man
Of this degenerate who despises you, and
Whom I despise and you often adore,
But I will not rebuke thee, dear.

ELI.

For six long days have we been in this place,
Our house all gone and of our stock,
Not one remains. My soul! There is no hope.
Heaven is closed and Negro men must die.
Ramech pray to your God.

RAMECH.

I have, and oft. But Eli we are doomed!

ELI.

And have we merited this fearful death,
This slow consuming agony, this famine,
Cold and pain, and O my God still more,
This inward consciousness of griefs stored up
For a long time yet! Look how our flocks
Are all swept off, our gathered crops;
Our children dead, but one, and we as outcasts

From our homes waiting for death to come
We were better off before Abe Lincoln freed
    us.

JOBEL.

Mama, I am hungry. Have you no bread?
My feet are wet and cold.

RAMECH.

My precious child! I have no bread.
O God protect my child!

JOBEL.

Some bread mama, just a little bread.
My feet are so cold.

RAMECH.

(Falling on her knees)

O precious God!
Thou knowest the secrets of our hearts, Thou
Knowest my unworthiness. Not for myself
Ask I thy mercy, but for my child. Lord—
O spare my child, my precious child.
He hath not wronged the lynchers.

ELI.

Ramech, I dreamed last night that our
Long departed Ajax had got home, and
Though he left us before the war I feel
Somehow he's yet alive and will
Visit us before we die. Its thirty-five

Years since we've seen him, he's changed I
    know.

RAMECH.

Heaven forbid that he should come to us
While in this valley of sorrows.

ELI.

I see upon the river a skiff which
Contains a boy, an aged looking boy.
And from my heart he looks much like our
    Ajax.

RAMECH.

It can't be so, what, Ajax, Ajax
The lost boy—long before old
Abe did set us free! Eli you dream.

    (A long silence)

ELI.

That's him, he's coming to die with us.

    Ajax comes up.

RAMECH.

Ajax my boy! Whence comest thou?
Where have you been? Hast thou forgotten
    me?

    (Falls in his arms)

AJAX.

No mother, dear; how could that be?
Thank God we've met but near our family
    grave,

Father, ere this, is ripe in age. He was
In his sixtieth year when Grant fought so.

ELI.

Ajax, what have you son, we perish.

AJAX.

Nothing have I: big piles I had but
In this land of lynching what ever we have
We have not. The lynchers envied my
Success and it was left with me
To lose my life or my earthly wealth.
I took the one you see me with here.

ELI.

I'm old, I'm cold, I'm hungry, I'm dying,
I yield to all.

RAMECH.

Grieve not, we shall not die of
Hunger. Before another night the lynchers
Will be here. They want our blood
Because it is innocent blood. Lets not repine.

JOBEL.

Mother I'm sick, this ground is wet to me.

RAMECH.

To see thee suffer in the bloom of life,
Thou whom I watched and cheered to
See thee perish thus—O God—.

JOBEL.

Mama I'm cold—has the bread come?

RAMECH.

O for the days when as a slave I worked.
Thy life would then be spared. But Lincoln
Freed us. Why are we not free now?
Is Lincoln yet alive, and Grant? O God
Blot these remarks from my memory.

She weeps.

AJAX.

Mother, fret not o'er thoughts like these
Let us pray God and wait our doom.

RAMECH.

My Lord.   My infant child and I once
Thought that you were dead.   But tell me
How did you live, we waited long for
Thee to come but all in vain.

AJAX.

We parted—sold as mules.   You
With my father's owner, he in another drove.
And I in a disgraceful to some one else.
I kept up with you all, until
The mighty struggle came that freed
Us all and effaced your whereabouts.
I started out in search of you and
Prosperity.   I lived quite well but

Seeking higher still, the white man
Envied me, and hence my life was his
When he saw fit, and eighteen years,
I've wandered up and down this world
In search of one dear spot where I could
Rest in peace.   It must be
Here to die with you.   At first
I feared to land.
O God, this lynching world is full of sin.

RAMECH.

Despite our griefs, I will believe, dear boy,
That Providence hath brought thee here to
     me.
That we might die together.

AJAX.

Mother what awful sights I've seen—
I oft have wished that I had died when young,
Before this dreadful calamity. My blood
Don't move, my mind deranged turns, at
     what
I've seen this day.   The carcases of
Men with that of oxen, sheep and hogs—
Did float together down the stream.
I saw two brothers take a stand for right
And there they stood, until the lynchers
Came—and made the one take the life

Of the other—murder his mother's son,
The one who did this work to save his life
Lay down exhausted.   Then the lynchers
　　took
His life by slow process and left him there.
The famished buzzards came to his rescue
And tore the quivering flesh.   In vain the
　　man
Fought this new foe till breath was gone.

ELI.

Didst thou see this?

AJAX.

That is not half.

RAMECH.

Then name it not.   I've heard enough.
I'm sick at heart.

AJAX.

I saw—my God I cannot tell.

ELI.

Tell on.   The woes of others told to us
May steel us to our own.

AJAX.

I saw a barge of logs loaded down,
With human beings, manacled, emaciated,
Ghastly. They sang and howled out prayers,

And curses and laughter. It was horrid.
With hands outstretched, they beckoned me
To come, but I stood off and watched
And heads of men were thrown at me in
  rage.
I further noticed a partly eaten body
Mangled and bruised. I shrieked aloud.
And then I saw a sight that captured all.
A mother, deathly clad, who in her arms,
Upheld a child. She cast her eyes on high,
And then she cast her infant from her.
It sank beneath the waves and was gone.
A mother drowned her own dear child.

RAMECH.

My God this lynching world.

AJAX.

Hush ? I hear the howl of dogs.

ELI.

My son, 'tis but the winds. No human
Being in this wild place save us. And the
" Star Spangled Banner" as that say goes
Doesn't wave here. Me think that song's
  a myth.

AJAX.

Again I hear the dogs. I'm not deceived.

15

Mother I dreamed last night I saw
A mountain moving on the waves,
And it had all the semblance of a house,
And my bewildered mind beheld unreal
  things.
By one of the windows I saw a
Gray haired man stand mute as death
And by his side I saw one young in years
His eyes toward heaven turned : and then
  again
He hid his face behind his hands
As if in sorrow.—And behold the old man
Turned his back to him.

ELI.

That means but this—that God in heaven
Has turned against us, and our doom is
  sealed.
And I will wait my hour in silence.
Fain would I curse, fain would I kill myself,
Would I could die !   Already have I lived
Too long—Hunger—Fear, my daily fiends!
Twelve days I've fought you bravely to be
Subdued at last by thee.

JOBEL.

How cold it is.

ELI.

Is that a human carcass floating on the
water?   Look Ajax, look!

AJAX.

The body of a lynched man.   Could I
But reach it, and eat once more before
I die.

ELI.

Go get it Ajax.   Thou art a swimmer.

(Ajax reaches the water and a band of lynchers rush
from the bushes and grab him.)

AJAX.

Oh father help me!   The devil has me.
The carcass had its spies.   Help!   Murder!

ELI.

(Rushes to his son's rescue, with his silvery locks dangling in his face. He rushes in their midst and grasps
his boy. The lynchers spear his aged body as if it was
a beast.)

Help, for I am stabbed.   My God these
Bloody lynchers—But wherefore call
For help when none can aid.   Ramech fare-
well!
Jobel, my child farewell!

(The father and son are lynched.)

RAMECH.

O Eli!   Ajax!   My God of heaven.

(She weeps aloud.)

JOBEL.

Mamma, why do you weep? Where is my
Papa?   Has he gone to get me some water?

RAMECH.

My precious child.   My husband and my son
Are gone and the lynchers will surely be
After you.   I hear them shriek for blood.
But I am nerved to die.

JOBEL.

Why don't my papa come?   I dreamed
He brought me some bread and you
Dear mamma and I were in a house.

RAMECH.

Sleep again my child, and in thy dreams
Forget the ills of earth and reign on high.
Oh God, please Thou forgive my sins,
And let me die; but Father spare my child!
He hath not sinned.   Hush! the lynchers
        come.
They took my husband and my son.
Ain't that enough?   Why trouble me?
I hear the howl of dogs.

JOBEL.

My papa won't come.   O mamma—

RAMECH.

My soul the lynchers are upon me!

O precious God! To Thee I yield my soul,
Do take my helpless child.
                    (The Lynchers rush upon her.)
My child! My own dear child!

JOBEL.

Mamma it is so cold. Have you
No bread for me? Where is my mamma?
Mamma—Mamma—Mamma.

*   *   *   *   *

But during this mighty struggle with
        Ajax and his foes,
He and one man fighting for life had
        drifted from the shore.
And Ajax fought a brave man's fight
        against a watery grave,
Exhausted down he seized some planks
        adrift upon the waves.
He stepped upon his rescu'd ship with
        clothes all dripping wet,
And blood from every garment fell, his
        eyes the white man's met.
Death had pressed him closely and
        precious was each second—
Two hands from out the water reached, his
        eyes toward Ajax beckoned.

There was the bloodless pallor of a wretched
    drowning man
With mouth all gaping, eyes bloodshot and
    hair on end did stand.
The struggling white man exhausted from
    trying to kill Ajax
Was fighting with water. now his strength
    was all relaxed.   ·
He cried "I perish my dear sir, give me a
    helping hand."
And Ajax's heart was melted down he drew
    him to a stand.
And Ajax said, "You've treated me as though I
    were a pup,
I give you good for evil—I in God's name
    bring you up."
And Ajax heard his mother shriek—afar upon
    the shore,
And tears gushed down his bleeding cheeks,
    "my God can it be so?"
The planks were drifting further and further
    down the river,
And Ajax turned to his shipmate and these
    words did deliver:
"The shrieking voice you hear comes from
    my mother's bleeding heart—

It is a shrill and helpless voice, it makes my
    senses start.
My mother murdered, butchered and my aged
    father slain,
Their infant child is murdered to, ought I
    silent remain?
Can it be true that I have saved your wretched,
    wicked life,
While others of your gang have killed my
    father and his wife?
You heathen of the white-skin'd tribe, you
    sit down there and wonder
I've robb'd grim death by saving you, your
    watery grave I've plundered.
I've prayed to God for vengeance through all
    these dreary years
I've gathered patience from my friends relat-
    ing all their fears.
My assailants have been many and my defend-
    ers few,
But now we stand as man to man, sir, should
    I murder you?
Grim death keeps secrets better than the mass
    of living men,
The river waves will gladly take you to the
    fishy den.
Then I could dive down in the waves and be,
    myself, at rest.

And your dear lynchers seeking me would
vainly beat their breast,
And though they are good hunters of the blood
of Negro's vein,
There they would follow—long and far to
ne'er find my domain.
Consider, as I do, sir, what the river's waves
would be
In contrast of the life, my peer, which now I
give to thee.
And I am now adrift, afloat in the marts of
the world,
And if the lynchers can catch me my soul to
wind'll be hurled.
If all the demons of your race could gather
'round us now,
Sir, all my pleading would not keep cold death
from my hot brow.
But man was made for life's battle, and sometimes life is fate,
To every man that breathes a breath death
cometh soon or late.
And how could you die better, sir, than by a
hand like mine,
For all my race's punishment by all your race's
crimes?

And could I die a nobler death than facing
    fearful odds

For vengeance of my father and my mother
    'neath the sod;

And for those tender mothers with their babies
    at their breast

Whose husbands died the death of dogs at
    your race's behest?

O! no, my mother's noble form lies not be-
    neath the sod,

Its now a prey for buzzards' feast, you wicked
    wretch! My God!

I have been at your mercy, sir, you tried to
    take my life.

I have no hope of your favor, for you I have
    no rife.

I could kill you and cast your form beneath
    the rolling waves

But I am human, so are you, I'm not to kill
    but save."

The white man set there calm as death he ut-
    ter'd not a word.

It seemed his frame was void of breath his
    soul was all bestirred.

He never gave an earnest look he did not even
    wink.

And Ajax said, "These circumstances do make
my conscience think.

O white man! have you any heart and did you
ever sigh,

And did your senses ever start to see a Negro
die?

Consider now the torture and the cruelty on
my race,

Look at my mother's cruel death, her infant
child effac'd.

Come go with me to Texas and see those red
hot irons—

That burn'd the eyes and mouths of men and
made them roar like lions.

And how the lynch'd men bellow'd like a cow
in deep distress,

And how the lynchers laugh'd and took it in
with minds at rest.

Oh! how the men did struggle to loose the
lynchers' chain.

Oh! how they howl'd like mad men, their efforts were in vain.

The guards had gone upstairs to rest, women
and children came

To view the scene with idle jest, and they were
not ashamed.

The angels 'round the throne of God had turn'd
    their backs to earth,
With hearts melted away in tears at sight of
    Texas mirth.
This land of brutal cowards still lack the moral
    backbone,
The moral courage, moral strength to drive a
    villian home.—
To even lift a finger or to raise a warning cry,
They stand in silent pleasure and gaze on the
    Negro die.
And in the shadow of the church human be-
    ings are burned,
From Sunday-schools the children rush this
    wickedness to learn.
They gather 'round to take a smell of burning
    human flesh,
They cheer the scene and make the spot a
    place of sacred mesh.
For him to plead, when all the hearts his
    keenest prayer could probe,—
Are but a breath of ether in the space around
    the globe.
It's no more than a ripple to the roaring water-
    fall,
It's a snow-flake in the valley to the cloud
    that covers all.

There's no protest, there's no rebuke, there's
    not a single cry —
Fished from the pools of blood and wrong to
    touch the nation's eye.
The world now sits in judgement and could the
    nations plead
This land would be a criminal of the vilest
    kind of deeds.
Could Ida Wells have raised a force to follow
    her crusade
This dreadful crime, long ere this time in
    darkness would be laid.
If Frances Willard and her host would help to
    raise the cry,
Intemperate lynchings ghastly ghost would
    fade away and die.
For when a woman makes a vow that she will
    do a thing
She's sure to win, or else she'll make oppon-
    ents conscience ring.
Few men of crime can stand to break a wo-
    man's heart, perchance,
Some nations chang'd their ship of state upon
    a woman's glance.
Fair Helen seal'd the fate of Troy and queens
    of ancient times
Have led brave hearts in cause of truth and
    made the wrong decline.

Some noble, stalwart woman have in every time
    and place,
Wielded her influence, good or bad, upon the
    human race.
If all the noble women who have a Christian
    heart,
While sitting by the fireside would take an
    active part,
And have a gen'ral family talk about the ship
    of state,
And speak of what the states should do to
    have a union great--
And speak of how almighty God was looking
    from the sky—
Down on the doings of each one. He heard
    the lynch'd man's sigh,
More husbands and more sons will go away
    from sacred homes—
With purer thoughts and higher aims and of
    a Christian tone—
'Till ships of church and ships of state will all
    be fill'd with men
With Christian hearts, with humane minds,
    with works oppos'd to sin.
Then there'd be more McKinley hearts as
    governors of states,

To see that men obeyed the laws which they
　　themselves would make
Then ev'ry gov'nor would be fit to make a
　　president
The white house then would ever have a man
　　with good intent.
Then lynching crimes would melt away as ice
　　in summer's heat,
Then we could praise this ship of state, this
　　union strong and great.
For many years my race has been a universal
　　target,
They never try to find the part that's crimson,
　　bright and scarlet,
In all of the affairs of life enormous fads have
　　spent
All of their forces upon him to bring our dis-
　　content.
All those unhappy phrases they should try to
　　set aright,
Are dwelt upon with mighty force to make as
　　dark as night,
A just investigation, to show the brighter side,
Is never made by those who strive forever to
　　deride.
The Negro's moral standard, sir, has never been
　　as low

As those destructive lyncher's hearts who nev-
er try to know
Whether it was a crime or not they're simply
satisfied
To pass their own meek judgment, they crave
the Negro's hide.
There's no class in America whose moral
pathway's fill'd
With thorns as is the Negro's and he must
tread at will.
American Christianity's not recognized by
Him
Who came to earth to die for man and give
him Christian trim.
Her body's broken by disease her conscience
seared with crimes,
A mind and soul of cruelty to cap the heath-
en climes.
And in the light of all these things it is a poor
spirit
To point with Christian horror but ne'er try
to prohibit.
Ah! what a reckless nation, what an undiscip-
lin'd child
Noble, but sometimes tricky, doing somethings
that are wild.

* * * *

A freeman am I, must I die a slave adrift at
    sea,
Or must I live as master's dog to whimper at
    his plea.
And must I crawl down at his feet, and must
    I lick his hands?
Poor Ajax' cheeks did flush with heat he
    ground his teeth like sand.
By Jove, by thunder, by the gods, I'd rather
    herd with wolves,
And seek the lion's friendship and to tigers
    make my love,
Then I could marshal all their strength against
    the cursed mob,
And teach them how it felt to give a beast a
    wailing sob.
To all my sorrows I would add those of my
    punished race,
And devote myself to vengeance upon this black
    disgrace.
And I would pray to all the gods, the gods both
    good and bad
To lend me their special terrors to ridicule this
    fad.
I'd ask for tempest, heat and cold, for drought,
    for wild beast's lair,

And all the poison of the land that men let
    loose in air—
And all the thousand other things that quickly
    put to sleep—
Of which men die on sea and land, my God!
    why should I weep?
My feelings are not vagary as a sensitive lad
But reas'ning of suffering manhood to give
    endurance sad.
Every age has its sorrows and O, the ills of
    time,
No parallel in human life to match this lynch-
    ing clime,
My spirit never goes to sleep I cannot rest at
    night,
A dog remembers, long, a wrong, he knows a
    friend at sight.
I have a book of great events, I'll write this
    voyage down
That men may know what I have seen and try
    its depths to sound.
My mother, father all are gone and I in this
    wild wood,
My wife and child sev'r'd from me, all gone
    but my manhood.
I never hope to find them now amid my anx-
    ious fears

As "Ben Hur" found his jewels after eight
    long grieving years.
He found his precious mother and his sister
    with disease,
From out a wicked dungeon he brought them
    to release.
But dungeons where the lynchers place the
    prison'd corpse of man
The buzzard sailing in the air has all at his
    command.
O white man! Can't I probe from you a single,
    tender sob?
And won't you help me pray one prayer to
    your Almighty God?
"O God! give me a little faith and into my
    darkness—
That's deeper darkening every day, O send a
    light of rest.
All hopes deal with the future Lord, I hope
    for better days,
And while I'm drifting down the tide, guide
    me the right of way."
Laurels of this world may be sweet but they
    soon pass away.
We have no laurels as a race, are they in com-
    ing days?

Like those colossal tombs of old on drifting
    desert sands

They cast shadows 'cross the cent'ries then
    crumble to the land.

This country in a prosperous stage will yet
    come to a halt,

And see the depths of this outrage and remedy
    the fault.

When time lies down fore'er to sleep at eter-
    nity's feet,

And vanities, pomps, more creep upon the
    stage so sweet—

And stars of heaven have all gone out of their
    ethereal home

The eternal hand, unseen by us across this land
    will roam.

        *   *   *

The evening shade was gathering now, the
    surging waters roll'd,

And Ajax felt the cool night wind, it seemed
    to fan his soul.

Unruly winds began to cease and zephyr's
    breezes rose

The lotus plant from water's depths before
    his gaze reposed.

The solemn river loiter'd on its way quite un-
    concerned.

The palm trees shook their nodding heads and
    stoop'd to greet the fern.
The Jackall slipping on the bank knew Ajax'
    skin was black
He snapp'd his teeth he thought t'was law his
    fleshless bones to crack:
The guiding stars began to show, the day went
    into night
And like a phantom ship at sea they drifted
    out of sight.
The planks, call'd ship on which they rode,
    went calmly down the river—
And no one knows unto this day which was
    the longest liver.
Did Ajax kill the white man? O no, his heart
    was tender!
Did white man kill poor Ajax? his heart was
    rash as timber!
Did both of them drift to the gulf and make a
    feast for whales;
Did both of them escape and shall we yet hear
    both their tales?
If poor Ajax is yet alive and dwells upon the
    land,
He'll write a book to shake this world and
    make men understand.

Dominus Vobiscum.

CONTENTS.

PART SECOND.

PART THIRD.

www.ingramcontent.com/pod-product-compliance
Lightning Source LLC
Chambersburg PA
CBHW030403270326
41926CB00009B/1252